WHO'S THE
Slow Learner?
Adventures in
INDEPENDENCE

To Nora
I hope you
have many
Adventures in
Independence!

Sandel
SANDRA ASSIMOTOS MCELWEE

outskirtspress
DENVER, COLORADO

Dedication

I dedicate this book to all of my fellow family members of the *Extra Chromosome Club*. I love how we support each other, argue but don't hold grudges, and stand by each other in advocacy. I am truly blessed by our association—and thankful I gained entry into this exclusive exceptional club on the day that Sean was born.

In Memory of
Ethan Saylor
Gregg Crawford
Kathy Ratkiewicz
Craig Keller
Patricia Minton

Acknowledgments

Kathie Olivier, thank you for the advice to not chase Sean when he was a young runner.

Miss Mo (Maureen Terrio) and Mr. Larry Green and Mandy Terrio, thank you for caring enough to stick with Sean for 4 years of Sunday school classes, providing him a strong base in his Christian faith.

Patty Miller, you were so accepting and open to Sean being a greeter with you at Saddleback when he was so young. It's great to see you every Sunday morning still welcoming people to our church.

Terri Green, your support, advocacy, and amazing sisterhood over many years provides me with so much inspiration.

Sandy Leifer, thank you for thinking up the creative title for the personalized books we created to introduce our children with Down syndrome to their typical peers in their inclusive classrooms.

Neighbors Dan and Cari Trimper, Patti and Jeff Wright, Scott, Donna, Brook and Brianna Kather, Joe and Mary Pasquariello, Don and June Silber, Rod, Michelle, Cameron and Cassie Turner, Bill, Pam, Megan and Katie Schley, without all of your wonderful support, encouragement and love of Sean we would have only dwelled in our home. Because of you all, our neighborhoods were true sanctuaries and a lot of fun too.

Gretchen Montgomery, thanks for being the best Cub Scout Den Mother any boy could want.

Dr. Wanda Claro, Dr. Ghafouri, and the Irvine Orthodontics staff, thank you for your unbelievable patience with your patient Sean. You gave him a dazzling smile and a lifetime of great oral health.

Lawrence Leightman, thank you for your dedication to the medical well-being of people with Down syndrome and the additional time you spent studying the nutritional and cognitive studies.

Many thanks to Sean's team of physicians starting with the one who birthed him, Susan A. Mendelsohn OB/GYN, best pediatrician ever; Mary Ann Wilkinson, MD; optometrist Robyn Rakov, OD FCOVD; ENTs John Supance and John Sun; and the cast of other specialists we have seen over the years.

Darrell Burnett, thanks for starting the local Little League Challenger Division.

Challenger Baseball coaches, VIP Soccer, Pop Warner Challenger Flag Football—it's the same cast of characters season after season: Maarten Voogd, Gary Fitzpatrick, Derrick Pinnecker, Dave Giertych and, of course, Dad (Rick McElwee), thanks for teaching Sean games and for being able to laugh while coaching all of our kids around the field of dreams. And thanks to the many Team Moms who organized snacks and parties over the years.

Michael Pless of M&M Surfing School, thanks for having the insight to know why Sean hesitated to learn to surf and thanks for the expertise in getting him on his feet. Surf's up!

Thanks to the volunteers of the U.S. Adaptive Recreation Center in Big Bear, California. Snow and waterskiing weren't Sean's cup of tea, but it's very good to know that he had the opportunity to learn from such amazing people giving their time for people with disabilities.

Laurie and Rich Jimenez, thanks so much for starting the Shooting Stars Basketball League.

Marty LaRoche, Steven Puck, Bucky and Sara Kahl, and Larry Wahl and Tijeras Creek Golf Course—thanks so much for the amazing golf program you have kept alive through much controversy and challenges. Sean has loved every minute of the program.

Tish and Gene Witkin, thank you for your countless volunteer hours. I am honored to know people like you who give so much, and don't even have a family member with a disability.

Sensei Wayne and Karate For All, thanks for working with Sean and helping him to achieve his black belt. He is very proud of that accomplishment.

Terrie Gero-Smead, thanks for all the years of organizing the best summer bowling league ever.

Terri Couwenhoven, Brian Chicoine, Dennis McGuire, and Kathie Snow, your books have been our guideposts in this journey to independence. I love hearing you speak at conventions. Thank you for your dedication to people with disabilities.

Buddy Sitters Ayden Loeffler, Kyle Olinger, and A. J. Borland, Sean loved coming home with you guys every day, and Chris Loeffler, it was amazing and so appreciated that you drove them every day.

To the Fries', Buckley's, Delayo's, and Davies'—your families embracing Sean has meant so much to us.

The Down Syndrome Association of Orange County and Director Kellie Perez—thanks for bringing the Lose the Training Wheels Bike Camp, providing Sean several opportunities to volunteer and being such great advocates for people with Down syndrome and for your amazing support for their families.

Kathleen McFarlin and Scarlett Von Thenen, thank you for your roles in supporting people with disabilities.

Area Board XIII, United Cerebral Palsy of San Diego, and Point Loma Nazarene University, thank you for including Sean in the first San Diego College Bound program.

Jan Weiner for all of your guidance and support since the beginning.— I still laugh thinking that you were the one who introduced us to Inclusive education when Sean was three months old and I didn't realize that was YOU until after the first book was published.

Joseph Nacario your patience and kindness is unequaled.

Kelly McKinnon and Kimberly Orliczky, you are the best behavior analysts ever. You both helped Rick and me to see that Sean's behavior was a form of communication and taught us to interpret his actions to understand his feelings. You both helped Sean to understand better ways to behave, and he trusts you both. Kimberly, your help with Sean's relationships really made dating less drama-filled . . . although I don't think dating will ever be drama-free.

Eric Latham, thank you so much for spending time with us on more than one tour of the UCLA Pathway Program visits. Your dedication to adults with intellectual disabilities is spectacular. And thank you for writing the forward to this book.

Saddleback Kids Sunday School Ministry, Amy Kendall, Todd Rolph, Sally Goodall, Vicky Burke, Paola Alvarez, Aurea Hernandez, Joelle Curtis, Zackariah Schuster, Stephanie Soofi, Katelyn Burke, Emily Boyer, and Jenni Warren, thank you all for serving with Sean every Sunday and teaching him to care for the children attending your classes.

Becky Rico, thanks for being the best magician's assistant ever!

Ashley Leo and Megan Schley, you both were great friends to Sean and helped him gain more independence through your support and friendship. Megan, thank you for teaching Sean to ride the public bus home from school.

Carlene Mattson, Andy Bean, Dave Donahue, Gracie Williams, Jean Beck, and all of the volunteers for the National Down Syndrome Congress Convention's Youth and Adult Conference each year gave Sean the opportunity to gain more confidence and freedom.

I can't even begin to name the many young adults who volunteer for Young Life's Capernaum and High Rollers' Clubs and now Refuge. Sean has been blessed to know you all. When he goes to the club each week he comes home confident and happy. Jesus' love shows on your faces and in your hearts, and we are all so blessed to know you.

Amanda Bacopulos and Lonna Albert at South Coast Freestyle thank you for starting DanceAbilities. And thanks to the dance buddies Thea, Lily, Zoie, Christa , Jax, Koko & Leah, you all rock!

To the many drivers Sean had who gave Rick and me our life back and kept me from experiencing every date he went on—Megan Schley, Bree D'Aleo, Ashley Silver, Chad Richards, Phillip Johnson—THANK YOU.

To the parents of Sean's girlfriends, thank you for your patience while we learn how to support our young adults in relationships. I am glad we can still be friends even after the breakups.

Paula Giertych, thank you for starting Cool Club with me. It was a great time every weekend.

Gail Williamson and Down Syndrome in Arts and Media (DSIAM), the positive awareness of people with disabilities provided by your coaching to producers, directors, casting directors, and all media is priceless. Our community is blessed to have you leading the way.

Brett Eastman, we so appreciate the whole experience you gave us during Sean and his friends' baptism. You made the day special for us all.

Rod Turner, your voice impressions of Santa Claus and Mike Scioscia helped us immensely.

Pam Patterson, SOAR is a great Adaptive Recreation Program and Sean has begun to enjoy everything you offer. Thanks for having the insight and caring for the health and fitness of adults with disabilities.

Keri Buckley, Heidi Fries, Pam Schley, Uncle Bob, and Todd Rolph, thank you so much for helping to move Sean into his new apartment. And to Jessica Fries, all you did to prepare Sean's home was a labor of love truly appreciated. Heidi Fries, your help in moving and your lifelong friendship has meant the world to us.

Cindy and Dave Brown, Jim Ragsdale, Mark, Erin, Gary and Kaysie Fitzpatrick, Brian, Melinda, Chris and Kevin Luttrell, your support and friendship in so many areas makes life more fun doing it together.

My beta readers, Michelle Hopkins, Dawn Thomas McNeil, Mary Erickson, Bill O'Dea, Alicia Elfelt, Renee Lovell Chambers, Renee Boyles, and Christine Hawkins, your input on this book was priceless and was a great help.

Ben Golden, thanks for being Sean's best friend. You two understand each other more than anyone else ever will. Kristi Golden, thanks for taking this journey with us.

Contents

Foreword

It Takes a Village . . .

"Children exist in the world as well as in the family. From the moment they are born, they depend on a host of other 'grown-ups'—grandparents, neighbors, teachers, ministers, employers, political leaders, and untold others who touch their lives directly and indirectly."

While not a new concept, Hillary Rodham Clinton's 1996 book cemented into our cultural parlance the role the village plays in the upbringing of our children. She illustrated the positive and negative impacts that many individuals and groups outside the family have on our children's lives. The challenge is harnessing those influences and combining them with the love and support of families to ensure our children grow into full, rewarding lives.

Parenting is hugely rewarding and very tough work. Every parent aspires to give their children a childhood full of wonder, passing on values and traditions while teaching, guiding, and supporting them through the highs and lows. The ultimate goal: self-reliant independent adults.

Independence, though, is a misnomer. What we typically value as independence is really interdependence—mutual reliance and responsibility to one another. This is the role of the village—to be the arena of formal and informal support that maintains the foundations of our society and culture. Though many debate how large or small the role, or who should be included outside of the family, it is undeniable that we all rely on our village.

Of course, the village and the systems it creates are flawed and do not always work as intended. Systems designed to help a broad group of people do not always work for those with very specific needs. The individual experience can be very different than the intended societal benefit. In my career working with individuals and families experiencing intellectual and developmental disabilities, I see these flaws most acutely with parents and families raising a child with a disability.

For better or worse, having a child with a disability increases your interaction with professionals associated with a myriad of specialized educational, medical, therapeutic, and social services. My entire professional working life has been in and around those systems. At its best I have seen multiple parts of the system work together to support a young woman requiring twenty-four-hour physical assistance to get her doctorate in psychology. At its worst, I have seen the system fail miserably—ignoring, covering up, and condoning abuse, neglect . . . and worse. Fortunately, positive examples from my career experiences far outnumber the negative. Much more common are stories I hear of parents stymied by bureaucratic and legalistic machinations designed to discourage them from asking for more or different services. Too often they are exhausted into compliance and submission to the status quo.

As a parent I share the desire and drive to give my children every advantage. I also know that as a professional, I have a different set of motivations. It is not an uncommon situation; we all have examples in our lives where we know what it is like to be on the other side of a relationship. All parents have experiences as children, and most bosses know what it is like to be an employee; the same can be said for teacher/student, doctor/patient, parent/professional—yet, we still struggle to understand and empathize when the roles are reversed.

Through fortunate happenstance, most of my career affiliations have been with programs and organizations initiated by parents of children with disabilities. My first job out of college was for a San Francisco Bay Area nonprofit created by a group of parents fighting to keep their children out of state institutions. When I moved to Eugene, Oregon, I worked for an agency bearing the names of the two founding families that successfully supported formerly institutionalized individuals with disabilities to live independently in the community. In Seattle, I worked for the United Cerebral Palsy Association, originally started by a group of moms because the public schools refused to teach their sons and daughters.

In my current position, I am director of Pathway at UCLA Extension, a program developed by a group of parents who wanted their adult children to have the opportunity to participate in college. Tired of the system's chronic low expectations and dissatisfied with the substandard transition and day programs available, these parents sought to create a new alternative, an opportunity for education, independence, and employment. Well ahead of their time, their efforts led to a growing movement of colleges and universities creating supports and programs for students with intellectual disabilities.

There are, of course, many examples of the village working together successfully, and, like all relationships, it takes effort and practice. We cannot continue to deny requests for support just because they are too expensive. We need to move beyond the liabilities and impracticalities of doing something that we have never done before. If we want to support independence we have to give up control and entrust others with responsibility. We need to get unstuck from what we cannot do and do the right thing.

Adventures in Independence is the story of Sean McElwee's journey into independent adulthood. It is a story unique to Sean, his parents Sandra and Rick, and the village that supports him, but it is also a story recognizable to many. It is about the love of parents willing to do whatever it takes to make a better life for their son—told through a series of poignant and often hilarious anecdotes. It is also about how all the well-meaning intentions of professionals are just that, and too often end up making things more difficult. This book gives me, and hopefully many others, an important reminder that our individual decisions and collective systems have an impact on real people.

Yes, it takes a village, but sometimes we villagers just need to get out of the way.

Eric M. Latham, MPA
Director, Pathway at UCLA Extension

Introduction

Kids respond to responsibility. Having talked to many parents over the years and seen this in my own life, I believe that it's far better to err on the side of giving too much responsibility than not trusting your kids enough. They're going to make mistakes either way. —Pastor Rick Warren

"I'm going to stay up all night." Sean crossed his arms and planted his feet, determined to win the argument this time.

"What are you going to do all night long?"

"Play Wii."

"No, you will be too tired and grumpy tomorrow."

"I won't. I promise. I can do whatever I want to. You aren't the boss of me."

"When you move out and live in your own apartment, then you will be the boss and you can stay up all night if you want to, but you still live in my house, so I make the rules. Bed by nine o'clock."

"Nooo! It's Friday, ten o'clock! When do I get to move out?"

"All right, ten o'clock." I turned and walked away, proud of the independent streak Sean was exhibiting.

As Sean traversed the rebellious teenage years we frequently had conversations like this one. He was expressing his desire to make his own rules, to be independent of his controlling parents. I appreciated the natural progression of his development, even though we had some of the same arguments I had experienced with my mother in my teenage years. Rick and I set the expectations that he would one day be living independently.

Sean is an only child. When he was 2 years old, I started lobbying for a second baby, and it turned out Rick and I had different ideas of what our family would look like. He only wanted one child, and since I am not a single-cell organism capable of agamogenesis, I had to learn to accept that I would only have one child.

Rick's family moved to California after he had graduated from high school, but one by one returned to Ohio and the East Coast.

I had moved to California from Texas without knowing a soul. I left several first cousins in Texas. My sister and her family moved to the East Coast.

Sean has no first cousins east of the Rocky Mountains.

No siblings, no close family, and with the average life span of a person with Down syndrome currently over age 60, the chances of Rick and I outliving him are slim. So independence is not just a huge goal for Sean, it is a necessity.

Adventures in Independence is the sequel to *A Chronicle of Inclusion and Exclusion*. I didn't start out to write two books but quickly realized that school was not the whole story for Sean. His extracurricular activities, dating, and moving into his own supported living apartment screamed to be chronicled as well. A few stories are repeated from *A Chronicle of Inclusion and Exclusion* to connect and fill in the blanks for anyone who didn't read it. This book completes the whole picture of growing Sean up to be independent. We frequently talked about "One day when you move out" to mentally prepare him that he would one day move out. When Sean wanted to do something and I didn't want to do it, I would say, "One day when you move into your own apartment you can do that." It was a constant conversation and a known expectation that he would one day move into his own home.

Many of the stories you will read in this book may prompt you to call Child Protective Services on us. We are fortunate to live in a small community, and because of Sean's inclusion in school and his many activities, he is known by many people in our community. The more people who know your child, the additional sets of eyes out in the community. I would not have given him so much freedom if we had lived in a large metropolitan area, or if we were nearer a freeway or other potential hazards. Who am I kidding, I didn't give him the freedom—he took it.

Occasionally I will see a report of a missing person who has Down syndrome. In the report the description makes me cringe as they say, "He is 16 years old but has the mental capacity of a 5-year-old." We were fortunate we never had to call the police to help find Sean, but I have friends who have had to do that, and it is nothing to be ashamed of. With today's technology, though, it shouldn't be necessary and as long as Sean doesn't turn his iPhone off, I can pinpoint exactly where he is at all times.

Since birth, Sean has had a magnetic personality and draws amazing people toward him—I call them angels. His very presence also can repel people who are narrow and prejudiced—I call them avoiders. Sean is a litmus test for character in others. Sean is very strong willed and determined, which serves him well when he is working to achieve a goal, and stands in his way when he is being rebellious against a person who may be trying to help him. He is also impulsive. He inherited his father's fantastic sense of humor, good looks, and athletic ability, and from me, his determination, tenacity, and friendly outgoing personality . . . and the inability to accept "No" as the answer to any question. We both function according to a combination of the "It's easier to gain forgiveness than permission" principle and the Nike tagline, "Just Do It." He learned that "No" doesn't mean "No"; instead, it constitutes the need to find an alternative way of achieving the objective. Tell Sean to hurry and he will stop, but tell him that you are racing and he will beat you. It's all a balance of being smarter than him, which isn't that easy to do.

Sean once told me he wanted to be a teacher. I responded, "You already are a teacher." Sean teaches people patience, tolerance, careful listening, creativity, and compassion. As for those who don't want to learn from him, he teaches *me* about their character if they openly reject his presence with bigoted words and actions. I particularly appreciate that lesson so I don't have to waste my time on the avoiders. Hopefully, you will learn from his adventures in this book.

We didn't do this alone. We had quite a few people who supported us. See the acknowledgments for a long list. In *A Chronicle of Inclusion and Exclusion,* I address behavior in much more detail. We had the help of behaviorists, both private and provided by Regional Center (the Department of Developmental Disabilities). Whenever you are at your wit's end, or have no clue what to do, please seek out the resources of professional behaviorists. The behavior techniques our parents used on us do not work with kids who have developmental disabilities. The most valuable lesson I learned is to use positive rewards instead of punitive punishments. When I consider this, I know I perform better in my work when I am rewarded than when I am punished and chastised.

Raising a young man who is respectful of girls, has good manners, and intentional boundaries was very important to Rick and me. Being that I was raised in Texas, teaching manners was a natural beginning for me. Sean was signing "please" and "thank you" before he could talk. All through school we received compliments on his manners from teachers and therapists. He always got a laugh when he was asked to do something in a therapy session and instead of some avoidance behavior, simply responded, "No, thank you."

We told Sean early on that he could date when he was 18 and get married when he was 30. That only lasted until high school when he saw couples kissing on campus and on dates at the football games and other school activities. We were busted, and he was allowed to date at age 15. Not that he ever went on an un-chaperoned date. Somebody had to drive them.

This is my memoir of Sean's journey to adulthood as we gave him more freedom and responsibility while learning what he was capable of achieving.

Health

I must say that there are worse things than being "disabled!" Having no compassion, no ability to see the value of a human being, having no ability to put yourself in another's shoes! These are the true disabilities!—Joni Eareckson Tada

The greatest medicine is not billable. It is not reimbursable. The greatest medicine is nothing that can be learned in medical school. The greatest medicine is hope. Although a doctor sees their patient as the child with Down syndrome, the parents must be considered patients as well. I have seen parents lose hope and stop trying for their child. If parents stop trying and the child's medical needs are neglected, then the child is the absolute victim.

Sean was at his 6-month well-check. He wasn't well. He had been constantly sick since the day he was born. During his birth he had ingested meconium and was diagnosed with pneumonia. He spent his first 10 days of life on intravenous antibiotics in the Neonatal Intensive Care Unit. One upper respiratory infection followed another, giving a nebulizer a prominent place on our kitchen table.

I presented the pediatrician a copy of the National Down Syndrome Society's Health Care Guidelines. He quickly glanced at the list of blood tests he needed to order and said, "This is way too aggressive. We don't need to perform all of these tests." Included in *all of those tests* were a screening for leukemia, which occurs frequently in Down syndrome, with no symptoms, *and* a thyroid screen. Sean was 6 months old. I told the doctor that the people who made that list knew a lot more about Down syndrome than I did and I wanted the tests done. (Today, the American Academy of Pediatrics has established these guidelines so primary care physicians are more likely to heed them. Guidelines for all ages can be found at www.ndss.org.)

A month later my friend took her son in to see the same pediatrician with the same checklist. She actually listened to the doctor when he said it was too aggressive. Consequently, her son was not tested. Two months later, bloated, lethargic, he was diagnosed with hypothyroidism. If the screening had been performed at 6 months, he would have been spared the health problems that come with untreated hypothyroidism, including slowed mental functioning.

Sean was born with pneumonia, and by the time he was 3 months old, he had his first bout of RSV, (Respiratory syncytial virus) and before he was 6 months old he had it two more times. Every 14 days we were in the pediatrician's office. Every cold turned into bronchitis or an ear infection or both. He could never just *get over* a cold . . . It always had to escalate into something else. He was on antibiotics for 10 days, off for 10, then sick again and back on them. By the time he was 2½ years old, he had been on antibiotics 45 times. He was quite the cash cow for his pediatrician and our pharmacy . . . a frequent flyer.

When Sean was 2½ years old I found out about Targeted Nutritional Intervention. I asked the pediatrician to look at the ingredients and give me his opinion. He said, "Well, there's not enough of anything to hurt him, but there's no proof it will help either." I asked him to see if he could find anything out about it in his medical journals and he said, "You know, 10 years from now and thousands of dollars later, none of this will make a difference."

I was speechless . . . a phenomenon that has rarely occurred in my life. I left his office fuming. As I buckled Sean into his car seat all I could think is, "Ten years and thousands of dollars from now—at least I can say I tried!" The reality was the $20 doctor visit copay and the cost of the antibiotics *were* costing me thousands of dollars, and making it impossible to work because no day care allows a perpetually sick child. So the constant illness was costing me more than some vitamins would. But more, it was costing Sean his ability to be fully present to learn, to develop, and progress to independence.

It is important to learn as much as you can about different therapies. I didn't want to discount the vitamin protocol without looking into it further. TNI (Targeted Nutritional Intervention) was, and still is, controversial in the Down syndrome community because some people have claimed it made their child smarter or more attractive. In Sean's case, it made him healthy. And guess what? There are all kinds of evidence that vitamins make us healthier. I made the decision we would not be seeing that pediatrician ever again and found one that had a nephew with Down syndrome, and continued her education surrounding Down syndrome and supported vitamin therapy.

When I looked into TNI more closely I found out there was a comprehensive vitamin panel available through Metametrix that could be performed to see what Sean's current vitamin levels were, so we ordered that test—with the new pediatrician. Sean had some very deficit levels in some nutrients and some very high levels in others. Six months after starting the vitamins we had him tested again and everything was in the normal ranges. We had him tested thoroughly every 6 months for a few years. Eventually we stopped the large panel testing, and when we had his annual thyroid screenings, we included testing for the fat-soluble vitamins A, D, E, and K. An excess of fat-soluble vitamins can have health consequences. (Note: Never start any vitamin program without a doctor's supervision.)

Once Sean began the vitamin protocol he only saw the pediatrician for well-checks. He never missed school because of being sick, and to be *IN* school you continue to progress; if you're constantly out of school, you can't learn. It's also tough to focus when you can't breathe or you feel bad because of a constant runny nose.

The hardest part of the vitamins at such a young age was it came in powder form, and it tasted pretty bad. Today, they have developed some different flavorings to mix with them so they aren't so disgusting, but we found mixing it in the individual-sized applesauce containers worked best for Sean. We just had to make sure he didn't have applesauce without the vitamins in it so he wouldn't know the difference. When he was 9 he said, "Mom, that tastes nasty." So I showed him how to swallow pills, and after that, it was much easier because he could swallow the capsules.

When Sean was 12—10 years after being told it would make no difference—I thought about sending that first pediatrician a video of Sean reading, doing his multiplication tables, throwing a football in a spiral a distance of 30 yards, hitting a baseball over the second baseman's head, and driving a golf ball straight down the fairway 100 yards . . . all without a runny nose. But I didn't have time for such nonsense when my healthy son had so many activities for me to take him to.

The same pediatrician also disregarded Sean's constant explosive diarrhea as simply a side effect of Down syndrome. Each time I asked him about why Sean would have so much diarrhea he repeated, "Children with Down syndrome have digestive issues." *But it is usually CONSTIPATION.*

Sean's diarrhea began the day after his first birthday. My parents were staying at our house and my mother had been a great help cleaning up after the party where over 70 of our friends had celebrated Sean's first birthday. I had returned to college and was taking evening classes, leaving as Rick came home from work. Rick was working late that day since my parents were able to watch Sean. I called to check on them during a break in my class.

"Is Sean up from his nap yet?"

"Oh, Sandra, is he ever. I went up to check on him and the smell hit me halfway up the stairs." My mother dramatically told me what happened next. "I looked into the crib and it was everywhere! Diarrhea. He had it in both hands, and was smearing it everywhere, and it was on his face. I screamed for your father. He ran upstairs, and I had him run the bath while I took the diaper off and carried Sean into the tub. The smell! I've never seen anything like it. I have the bedding in the washing machine now. Gag!"

That was the first blowout but far from the last. At age 3 we were transferred to Washington State for a 1-year project Rick was assigned to. The pediatrician there gave me the same answer: "Children with Down syndrome usually have digestive problems." Sean was impossible to potty train due to no control of his bowels and was close to turning 4 years old. The diarrhea had continued for *3 YEARS*. I scheduled another appointment and asked the pediatrician, "If he didn't have Down syndrome, what would you do after 3 years of diarrhea?" The answer, "Refer him to a gastroenterologist."

The first GI in Washington that we saw ordered tests. Lactose intolerance (which led to needle intolerance after the first two blood draws. It took three people to hold Sean, almost 4 years old, down for the third one). Next was the endoscopy to check for celiac disease. No celiac, but a discovery of silent reflux was present, and some damage to his esophagus had already occurred. Then we were transferred back to California. The next GI actually had her nurse play with Sean in the waiting room and interviewed me for over 30 minutes about his eating and drinking habits. Thirty minutes with a doctor. Sean was 4 years old, and I don't think I had ever spent that much face time with one medical professional before. She simply instructed me to not give him anything to drink but water and milk for 2 weeks, and keep his diet otherwise the same. After 1 week, Sean had a solid bowel movement. It was the juice. It was the sugar in the juice. How simple, and my son suffered for 3 years because I was too wimpy to question the doctors. OK, I suffered too. Those diapers were nasty, and most of the time there was overflow involved. Rick even had to buy a new shirt at Disneyland one day after experiencing some overflow.

Sugar in any form caused Sean to have diarrhea. Birthday cake was the culprit of the first episode after his first birthday party and the first cake he had ever eaten. I attended birthday parties with him, and when they served the cake I would scrape his icing off and make sure his piece was tiny. When there were school parties I had warned the teachers, but I knew when Sean got home if he had eaten cookies or other sugary treats. The evidence was inevitable. We made him aware when he had diarrhea that it was because he had eaten or drunk something with sugar in it. As a teenager he would project an announcement from the bathroom when he had too much sugar. "Too much sugar Mom!" But thankfully he had made it to the bathroom in time for many years by then.

Independence Begins Early

*I am no bird; and no net ensnares me: I am a free human being with
an independent will.* — *Charlotte Brontë, Jane Eyre*

Early Sunday morning, before the stores opened, Sean and I entered
the mall through the entrance next to the first anchor store. Not a soul
was to be seen as we began to walk toward the other end of the mall.
We only took about five steps before he bolted—and I ducked into the
doorway of one of the closed stores and hid. I could see him through
the glass display window, but he couldn't see me. He ran, and ran, then
started looking back over his shoulder with an expression that took me
by surprise—he was laughing and had his "I got you" mischievous look
on his face. The little stinker thought this was a fun game, and I realized
he was getting an endorphin rush from being chased.

He finally realized that not only was I not chasing him—I was
nowhere to be seen. He stopped, turned around and around, then sat
down and cried . . . and I let him cry for about 2 minutes. (That's a
long time to hide in a doorway letting your child cry—but I was pretty
sick of chasing him all the time.)

I finally emerged from the doorway and said, "Sean, you were
lost. I couldn't find you. Stay with me and you won't be lost again."
We walked to almost the middle of the mall, and he took off again. I
ducked inside a doorway again, he dropped to the ground, cried, and
I once again explained that he needed to stay with me so he wouldn't
be lost.

Sean was a runner. Once he started walking at 22 months old it took no time before he was running away from us. He was exerting his independence by breaking away from us at a very early age. He would frequently run away, running toward traffic, running through customers' legs at the mall—the shoppers thought he was so *cute*. I frantically chased him, unable to fit through the shoppers' legs myself, and panicked as he got further and further away from me. Nobody ever stopped him for me.

He ran out of class at school. We lost him once in the Chicago O'Hare Airport during Christmas holiday travel between flights. He ran away any time he had an opportunity.

I finally asked the psychologist from his Early Intervention Program how to get him to stop running. She simply said, "Don't chase him." Hmmm . . . tempting, but I would probably be in big trouble if I stood by as he ran in front of a car in the grocery store parking lot and was killed or maimed beyond recognition. She then suggested we go to a *safe* place and when he ran, not chase him there.

Well, it took a lot of thinking to come up with a *safe* place. I'm a pretty slow runner, and when Sean got enough of a head start on me there's no catching him.

One day I realized that the stores in our mall don't open till 11 a.m. on Sundays, BUT you can go into the mall and walk. So, one Sunday, when Sean was 4 years old, I drove over and let Rick out at the entrance to the center of the mall. (If Sean was going to run and I couldn't catch him then he'd be there to stop him before he got completely away.)

I thought we would have to visit the mall for a few more Sundays before he learned this lesson. But it was easier than that. The next day we were in a fabric store, and he was staying with me the entire way . . . *following ME.* It was the most pleasant shopping experience I had had in years. I turned a corner and for a minute was out of his sight, and he immediately began to cry. WHOO HOO! I thought he finally CARED that I wasn't there.

Now, I'd love to say that he never ran again—he never ran again from me, but EVERY time he encountered a new situation—a new teacher, aide, babysitter, etc., he would *test* them and run. If they *DID NOT* chase him, then he didn't do it again, but if they did, he would play the game. Then the hard part was teaching them not to chase him.

At school we asked them not to chase him when he would run out of class. And he ran out of class a number of times in kindergarten and first grade. The protocol was when he would bolt out of the room, the aide would go to the window to see which direction he was going. She discovered the little stinker would get outside and stand waiting for them to come after him, and when the door didn't open he would go back into the room and sit back in his seat like nothing ever happened.

I have to remind everybody that it takes two to play the game. If you simply don't play, the fun is gone and the game ends.

Singing and Dancing

There are short-cuts to happiness, and dancing is one of them.
—Vicki Baum

There wasn't a lot of entertainment in the area of Washington we were temporarily living in, but it seemed every weekend there was some sort of festival. Festivals for Vidalia onions, sausages, Memorial Day—the harvest of any food item or celebrated holiday was an excuse for a festival.

They always had several raised platform stages, and different groups provided entertainment. Square dancers, karate black belt demonstrations, cheer groups, and more.

Sean has always been a great audience member. One warm Saturday we watched this adorable group of 3, 4, and 5-year-olds singing and dancing. The children were adorable. The girls wore bright yellow floral dresses, and the boys had matching floral yellow shirts, black slacks, suspenders, and bow ties.

Sean was enthralled. We were seated on the front row in the plastic chairs that were carefully placed for the audience members. Sean stood in front of his chair and tried to imitate their dance moves and hand motions. As the performers were taking their final bows Sean looked at Rick and me and pointed at the children, *"DAT."* (That) Then pointing at himself, *"ME DO."* No question he was letting us know that he wanted to join this group.

I picked up a flyer that one of their members was handing out, and on Monday morning I phoned the director. "We saw your group performing on Saturday at the festival, and my son is interested in joining. He's 3½, has Down syndrome, is deaf in one ear, and really can't talk much. He can't carry a tune, but he can dance—"

Before I could finish my pitiful description she stopped me, "None of that matters. I have many special children in the Sunshine Generation. Bring him to rehearsal tomorrow afternoon."

Sean rehearsed every week and performed in the community about once a month with the Sunshine Generation, attempting to sing and definitely dancing—he had all the moves down. On stage he fit in perfectly with the rest of the children. During performances he would work his charm. He would pick some cute girl in the audience and blow kisses to her. He would emphatically bow at the end of each performance, certain that he was the only dancer that was being applauded. After every performance people sought us out and told us how Sean had touched their hearts. One family broke our hearts; they told us of their daughter who had been born with Down syndrome 10 years earlier. She had a severe heart defect and sadly she had not survived her heart surgery. Her family was still mourning her passing, and they wanted Sean to meet their daughter and son who were under age 10—they explained to their children that Sean was like the sister they had never known. It was very touching to us that Sean was inspiring so many people.

Sean's first inclusive experience was in that singing and dancing group. While he frequently was offbeat and occasionally a step or two behind the song, the other kids were too. He couldn't sing, so they placed him away from the microphones. He loved being on stage and took his role very seriously.

When we returned to California I enrolled him in our church's children's choir. They performed at church, in the community, and even at Knott's Berry Farm. Sean was a natural on stage, but with a 30-minute production he would get tired and sit down on the risers during the performance.

During the Christmas performance Sean was awarded the role

of a Wise Man during a re-creation of the nativity. The Little Lambs Choir began their songs. Backstage, Sean and his fellow cast members were in costume and ready for their cue. The Angel was already on stage with the rest of the choir and Joseph and Mary entered first, holding the Baby Doll Jesus, and took their places behind the manger. The Angel presided next to them. The Wise Men made their grand entrance bearing their gifts. For some reason the Angel had been wingless during dress rehearsal. And then Sean noticed it. The Angel had on tinsel-rimmed wings. He was enthralled and couldn't stop staring at her wings, the expression of awe on his face was priceless . . . and then he had to touch them. He had to see what they felt like. He reached out and gently patted the wings and nodded his approval to the Angel. The laughter was uproarious.

The next year during the Christmas performance the choir director was brave enough to give Sean a place up front with four others in the lead singing, "All I Want for Christmas Is My Two Front Teeth." The four children all shared one microphone in front of the additional 50 children comprising the backup singers on the risers. Sean had other ideas though. He didn't want to share the microphone, his first opportunity for the spotlight. He kept pushing the other children away from the microphone while he was shouting, "Ah I wan for Ristmus is ma two Font Teef." He truly wanted a solo, not a shared spotlight. Once again, the congregation laughed at the adorable Sean fighting for his place in the spotlight.

Sean gained a lot of confidence performing in front of a few thousand people. I never saw one moment of anxiety when he was on stage. On performance days he was so excited and couldn't wait to take his place on stage.

I was in the audience. I couldn't stop him from touching the Angel's wings. I couldn't stop him from pushing the other children away from the microphone. I couldn't walk him back to his place on the risers during another concert when he left his position and decided he was going to stand next to the choir director and imitate her arm and hand movements while conducting the choir. I had to learn to give him his independence. Even though he didn't always make the best choices, I had to loosen the reins and give him his space so he could exercise his wings of independence.

Church Inclusion

Whatever you did for one of the least of these brothers and sisters of mine, you did for me. (Matthew 25:40, NIV)

Sean began attending church when he was less than a month old. First we kept him with us in the adult service, and as he grew into Sunday school we took him to his age-appropriate classes.

During our 1-year stint in Washington State we visited around five churches before we found one that resembled our California church home. We found one that we really liked and Rick and I had decided that was where we would attend—until we picked Sean up from the 3-year-old Sunday school class and were informed that he would have to go to the 2-year-old class because he was still in diapers.

Church lasted less than an hour and a half, and while we had issues with diarrhea Sean was not a morning pooper. I assured them they would never have to change a diaper, but the leader was adamant that he could not be with his same-age peers. So we continued to look for a church home. This was the first time I had experienced any sort of bias toward Sean. People aren't perfect; some just follow rules without being aware that accommodations are the norm for people with disabilities in every area of life.

We found a nice church the following weekend that embraced Sean and who were thrilled to see him each week.

Returning to California the following year, Sean was in the 4-year-old Sunday school class, and still in diapers, but nobody had a problem with that. The following 2 years (since he attended kindergarten twice), he was in the kindergarten Sunday school class. His Sunday school teachers, Miss Mo and Mr. Larry, were especially kind and sweet. Sean would regularly dash out of class, and they quickly learned to anticipate when he was about to bolt out of the room and redirect him before he could escape.

One day as I picked Sean up he took off and escaped from me running between other parents' legs and disappearing. We were searching everywhere, and the Sunday school supervisors had radioed everyone to look for Sean. We realized he must have ducked into another classroom when he was nowhere in the common areas. I went back to the classroom area and saw a woman walking out of a classroom holding his hand. She had placed a name tag on him that said, "John," and she was taking him to the office to see if she could find his lost parents. Sean's articulation was almost unintelligible. That she was able to decipher "John" was pretty good.

Sean had a horrible habit of testing new teachers. Every year when school started he would be really good the first few days, then he would start testing his teacher. He would run out of class to see what reaction he would get. He would get into a classmate's possessions inside their desk. Looking for the boundaries, learning how the teacher would react and figuring out what he could get away with he was like the Velociraptors in *Jurassic Park,* looking for the weak place in the fence . . . Testing and testing until he knew what was expected of him.

Miss Mo and Mr. Larry were true godsends. They knew how Sean tested them the first year in kindergarten Sunday school. Only being in church once a week, it had taken him longer to learn the boundaries than it did in school. As Sean was transitioning into first grade they made the decision to move up from kindergarten and teach Sean's first-grade Sunday school class, and later, his second-grade class too.

One day when we were driving home from church we heard Sean in the backseat say, "God is Jesus." Rick and I looked at each other with our jaws dropped open. This was a rare occasion when

Sean spoke clear enough to understand an entire sentence. I knew his Sunday school teachers were teaching him the most important truth that he would learn in his life.

The best part was I was able to relax and enjoy the message and music and never had to worry about what mischief he was making during services on Sunday. I was able to worship with a free heart and mind. Knowing he was with two amazing godly people who truly cared for him with mutual respect and trust, Sean was learning about Jesus from them.

Playing in the Pool

Life is like a swimming pool. You dive into the water but you can't see how deep it is. — Dennis Rodman

It was a hot August evening and I had promised five-year-old-Sean that we would go to our townhouse swimming pool after dinner. I pulled him in our red wagon the one block to the pool and entered the gate. He climbed out of the wagon and walked quickly to the stairs, climbed in with me right behind him. The water felt nice and cool on our hot dried out skin.

Our neighbor David and his two children were also in the pool and playing. David was picking them up and throwing them towards the deep end. They laughed and swam back to him, "Do it again, Dad!"

Sean was entertained and looked at me with a question of permission pointing to himself, "Me do?"

I got David's attention, "Sean wants you to throw him too."

"Sure Sean. Come on over."

Sean swam over to David. David is pretty muscular and easily lifted Sean's little body up and out of the water and tossed him into the deep end.

Sean hit the water...awkwardly...crotch first...and when he came to the surface I could tell he was in pain, his tiny testicles were racked.

Gasping for air, his bottom lip quivering, he was doing his best to hold back the tears. He made his way back to the stairs. Sitting on the top stair, in about 2 inches of water he pulled the elastic waistband of his swim trunks away from his stomach to see for himself. He looked down, then looked at me and choked out, "He broked it."

Hugging Sean to comfort him I couldn't stop myself from laughing. I wasn't laughing at his pain but, "he broked it" was the funniest thing I ever heard anyone say.

David holds a high position in our church and Rick and I chuckle every Sunday when we see him—16 years later— and laugh together, "He broked it."

Self-Awareness

The better you know yourself, the better your relationship with the rest of the world. —Toni Collette

Before Facebook existed I was a frequent participant in an Internet Parent Support Group—The Down Syndrome Listserv. One day a sibling posted advising us parents that we tell our children that they have Down syndrome early. She told us the story about her sister, who had a visit from a social worker when she was 14 years old to begin her transition planning.

The social worker was interviewing her and the sister asked, "Why are you asking me all these questions?"

The social worker responded, "Because you have Down syndrome, and we're planning for your transition to adulthood." Her sister was livid and stayed mad at her family for quite a while because they had not told her that she had Down syndrome before, and this stranger was the one who delivered the news to her.

From an early age I made sure that I told Sean that he had Down syndrome. I was adopted and can't tell you the first time my parents told me that fact; it was always a *normal* part of my life just knowing. I wanted Sean to know he had Down syndrome and for that to be a *normal* part of his life too. I couldn't imagine him being surprised by some stranger telling him when he was older.

Acceptance of yourself is critical to being a self-confident adult. Awareness of one's limitations and being able to communicate it to others is empowering and enables others to know what areas you need help with.

I would read him books that had characters with Down syndrome, then say, "You are just like the boy in the book. You have Down syndrome too." He began to recognize the facial characteristics of other children with Down syndrome.

I didn't expect him to be so enthusiastic about recognizing other people with Down syndrome, and he caught me off guard one day. We were attending an event at the local Down syndrome association, and Sean ran up to several children, pointed to them, and said in his inarticulate manner, "Thown Thyndome." I was laughing inside. I knew what he was saying, but thankfully, nobody else could understand his words.

I felt that it was important to educate the children in Sean's elementary school classes and their parents about Sean and Down syndrome. Fear comes from the unknown, so I wanted to make sure people weren't afraid of Sean, and educating them alleviated that fear.

In regular education kindergarten, I grabbed the first opportunity I had to educate his classmates and teachers. This letter went home with each student:

Dear Parents of Mrs. _____'s Students,

The theme of this year's "Red Ribbon Week" is disability awareness. Since our son, Sean, is in your child's class and has a disability, it seemed appropriate to make the children aware of Down syndrome. We are sure many of your children have asked you questions about Sean, and that is great. We have two copies of a really good book titled, *Hi, I'm Ben . . . And I've Got a Secret!* The teacher will be sending it home with two different students each day so you can read it to your child, then please send it back for another child to read tomorrow. This book answers many questions that children have about Down syndrome. It stresses that children with Down syndrome are more like them than different.

One big question that startles adults is, "Can I 'catch' it?" This is a very real concern that children have from age 4 to about 8 years old. The best way to alleviate this fear is to explain that you have to be born with Down syndrome, just like they were born with brown or blond hair. They can't "catch" Down syndrome just like they can't "catch" blue eyes. Please take a moment to read the first two pages that are directed to adults before you read this book to your child. Then at the end of the book, you might ask, "Do you know anybody that is like Ben?" If your child says, "No," then it's fine to leave it there. But I am sure most of the children will pick up on the facial characteristics that Ben and Sean share. They will also relate to the speech teacher, as Sean's greatest challenge is his speech difficulty. Please remind your children that they are all Sean's teachers. Sean will learn as much, probably more, from your children this year than he will from his teacher and his aide. So it is important that they show Sean good things to do, because he will also copy the not-so-good things as well.

Thank you so much. This year has been a dream for us and is a greater success than we imagined it could be.

Rick and Sandra McElwee

P.S. Please feel free to call us with any questions. We do not get offended by anything. We've heard it all.

I showed the first-grade teacher the book *Hi, I'm Ben . . . And I've Got a Secret!* and told her one of my friends had made her own book. She thought the idea to create a book about Sean was a good idea because the kids could relate directly to him, and we could enlist their help with some behavioral issues he was having.

Sean's friend's kindergarten teacher, Sandy Leifer, had created the title, *My Name Is ____ and I Have Something to Share!* so we used the same title for Sean's personalized book. Using a computer, we scanned in photos of Sean with captions that explained different things about him that were the same and different.

One page said, "I like to throw rocks, but I need my friends to help remind me to leave the rocks on the ground." The school had removed all the grass and was reseeding it. There were dirt clods and rocks everywhere, and when Sean was outside, he would pick them up and randomly throw them. There was a very real concern that he might actually hit somebody with a rock, and he did throw hard. By including this behavior in the book about him helped to address the rock-throwing issue and enlist the help of his classmates. They took real ownership of watching to make sure Sean left the rocks on the ground. (I decided to publish this book. It's now available and includes the parent letters explaining inclusive education and facts about Down syndrome in the last pages.)

Sean's first-grade teacher visited the other three first-grade classes and read this book to the students. Sean was an instant celebrity.

Today, I encourage parents to create a personalized book about their children on their computer. It's easy and inexpensive.

Sean was not present when his teacher read the book. She waited until he went to speech therapy. She wanted the children to feel comfortable asking any other questions and didn't want Sean to feel uncomfortable . . . although he probably would have loved being the center of attention.

Neighborhood Independence

Ignorance is our greatest hope. People who know nothing about disability get it so much more than people who have been educated about disability—Ann Turnbull

Barney the Purple Dinosaur was my in-home babysitter. If I needed a shower, I knew Barney would keep Sean occupied so I could spend a few moments on my personal hygiene. We lived in an end-unit townhome that was attached to three other townhomes.

One day I came downstairs after my shower and Barney was singing, but Sean was nowhere to be seen. Major panic set in as I noticed he had left the front door wide opened. He was only 5 years old. I went out looking for him, stopped at the next-door neighbors to find they were not home and was at a loss of where else he would have gone. Then out came Dan, our neighbor from the unit at the opposite end of our units. Dan was a retired mailman around 6 feet tall, had a shaved head before it was gangsta, and he was a very funny guy.

He asked me, "Did you lose something?"

I responded, "Yes, I can't find Sean."

He was laughing. "I found him for you. Come check this out." Dan had also been showering and when he came downstairs had discovered Sean sitting in his recliner, footrest extended, watching his new big screen TV. I went in and there he was reclined, legs crossed, making himself at home. Thank goodness Dan thought it was cute. With someone else this could have been pretty dangerous. I told Sean that I needed to be with him when he went outside, and we added a door latch that was up too high for Sean to reach after that. I realized since he did this once it wouldn't be the last time. Especially with that giant TV as a temptation.

About a year later we moved into a single-family home on a cul-de-sac. It was a perfect neighborhood for Sean. Rick and I first looked at the house without Sean, and as we were leaving, around eight kids in Sean's age range were sitting on the curb checking us out. Sean was in first grade, and I recognized some of the kids from his school. There were 13 children living on the cul-de-sac, and this gave us the beginning of allowing Sean to have some independence.

The New Neighborhood

A good neighbor—a found treasure. — *Chinese Proverb*

As we had anticipated, the cul-de-sac turned out to be the perfect place for Sean to grow up. Initially, I needed to keep an eye on him to make sure he was being socially appropriate so I bought some fun outdoor toys that he and the neighborhood kids loved. We quickly became the house that everyone hung out at. Basketball on the drive-way, trampoline in the backyard. Slip-n-Slide during the summer . . . We bought plastic bats, balls, and bases to play baseball in the street.

In Southern California, land is a commodity, and nobody has a large yard, so the cul-de-sac provided a large enough space to allow everyone the space to play. There was a park around the corner, but we were not ready for Sean to go that far where I couldn't just look outside and see him, and I needed to be near home to cook dinner and do things around the house too.

As the children and their parents got to know Sean better, I would let him play without me outside supervising. There was always one mom keeping an eye on everybody, even though it was a pretty safe neighborhood. He continued to walk into people's homes if their front door was unlocked. We had to teach him to ring the doorbell and wait, then walk away if there was no answer . . . not open the door and go inside. He did let one neighbor's dogs out of the house, and the dogs were prone to running away, but they just surrounded Sean and wagged their tails while he petted them.

We had other kids with special needs on our cul-de-sac, and there was a disproportionate ratio of girls to boys, and Sean loved all of the girls. But they didn't cut him any slack. He had to behave just like everybody else, play by the rules, and take turns. Nobody got to take more turns than anybody else.

One of Sean's teachers told me that we needed to make learning colors meaningful to Sean because he simply wasn't learning them. During the summer between second and third grade, one of the girls on the cul-de-sac taught Sean his colors.

He was obsessed with handball. In the game of handball they used a ball that was used for dodgeball when I was in school. The ball is bounced off of a backboard at school . . . or off of the garage at home, and each person gets a turn at hitting the ball, bouncing it off the garage door with a specific bounce. The balls came in many colors, and they were cheap. I bought Sean every color, and one of the girls came over to play. She kept changing whichever ball she wanted to play with.

"Sean, let's play with the purple one now."

Sean would go over to the balls sitting on the lawn and have to figure out which one was purple. She did this with each color until he knew all of the colors of the balls. Make it meaningful . . . It worked. He needed to know the color in order to continue the game with a friend that was meaningful to him.

In spring of fourth grade Sean began walking to his elementary school with the other kids in our neighborhood. He was very proud of being included with them and didn't want me to drive him anymore. He was growing up, and I was letting him.

Sean was 10 years old when good friends of ours moved in two doors away. Their son has a developmental disability too, and he had played baseball on Sean's team. We let the two walk back and forth between our houses together. I was becoming very relaxed about Sean being in the neighborhood unsupervised. His speech was becoming more articulate, so he was able to tell me most of the time if something happened that I needed to know about, and, of course, the other children were happy to report back anything I needed to know of Sean breaking the rules or not taking turns.

Sean's fifth-grade best friend lived in a condo about four blocks away. One day his mother phoned me. "Did you know Sean walked to our house?"

Yikes. He had to walk four blocks into a condo complex that was kind of confusing to maneuver and locate their condo in a grouping where even *I* had to carefully look for their unit number when we went there. That was when I realized Sean could handle more independence, but I wasn't sure that I was ready yet.

That Christmas I got Sean walkie-talkies so he was able to call me and let me know where he was. We practiced in the cul-de-sac. He had to radio me every time he went to a different person's house and tell me where he was. He did a great job, and I let him walk the four blocks to his friend's house, and he radioed me from there. He was learning how to check in and a few times when he forgot I found him and made him come home as a consequence.

We had many parties for Sean's classes at our house; end-of-year parties, Halloween parties, and, of course, birthday parties. Because we had so many parties Sean's classmates knew where we lived and that we had a fun and welcoming home that they could come to. As they grew older they would ride their bikes over and hang out.

Fostering Classmate Friendships

Together we're better. Thank goodness we all need each other.
— Marsha Forest and Jack Pearpoint

One of the benefits of being fully included in your neighborhood school is living where the other students live. Sean met many kids at school that lived in the surrounding neighborhoods. I made sure to have a lot of fun things to do and play with and we had the house where all the kids hung out. Sean wasn't invited for play dates outside of our cul-de-sac very often. There were a couple of kids who really liked him, and I would go to the play dates with him at their houses the first few times and get to know their moms. Over time they became comfortable with Sean and how to react (or not react) to his testing behaviors.

In first grade I offered the idea of a class roster. The principal approved it. (There is a process in every school district for approval for anything to be sent home with the children. Learn that process before offering this.)

I made a roster, and it was sent home with every child so they would have each other's name, phone number, and address so we could see who lived only a block or two away and would be easy to invite over without their parents having to drive them. We also hosted "End-of-School Parties" each year at our home or at a community pool and offered the teachers the ability to have the class plan the parties as a school activity. An ulterior motive was so the parents would feel comfortable having their children come to our house, and that they would know us and where we lived too. Collaborating with the teachers, we made the party a learning experience for the students too. Here are the instructions provided for the first-grade End-of-School Party:

End-of-School Party at Sean McElwee's House for (teacher's name) First-Grade Class

I am sending an Oriental Trading Co. magazine for the kids to look through. If they want to play games with prizes they can choose the prizes, plan the games, etc.

If they want food, they need to find out how much it will cost, how much they will need, and the same for drinks. Do they want their parents there too? They will need to include their food and drinks as well.

Do they want a bounce house or one of those blow-up slides? If so, they will need to find out where to order it, and how much it will cost.

We will pay half of the cost of the party up to $100. So, after the students come up with their costs, and then divide it between everybody who will be able to come, they will know how much it will cost each student to attend.

We can have the party the last day of school after school, or the Saturday following the last day.

So, plan away and let me know what the kids come up with. Oh . . . If they need to come and tour the party facility in advance, they are welcome to come to see what we already have as far as games and fun here.

THANKS.
Sandra McElwee

As Sean got older we hosted Movie Nights in our living room. Although we invited the whole class, not everybody would come. But everybody who did come had a great time. Here's one of the invitations we sent to the class.

Sean McElwee Invites you to

McElwee Movie Night!

Feature Film:

The Wild Thornberry's Movie

Saturday, May 31st

5:00 till 9:00

Hot Dogs and Hamburgers will be served

Please RSVP by Friday, May 30th
Sandra McElwee
Phone number

I didn't expect a lot of parents to invite Sean to their house, and I wanted to make sure our home was welcoming and fun for his classmates to come to play. Relationships built outside of school or in other situations solidify school relationships significantly. I wanted Sean to have the opportunity to have some solid friendships established early.

Haircuts from Hell

No pressure; no diamonds.—Bear Grylls

Due to sensory issues, haircuts were traumatic experiences for me—oh, and for Sean too. We were lucky to have a children's hair salon close by who specialized in the "quick haircut." Not cheap, but quick. Rick or I had to smock up ourselves, then hold Sean on our laps and hold his hands down while they quickly trimmed up his locks. In kindergarten, Sean made a good friend named Jeffrey. He loved Jeffrey, and Jeff's mother even invited Sean to come and play at their house. They lived close by, and she became a good friend of mine too. As the school year was ending, Jeff got a summer buzz cut, and Sean was enthralled with it. He came home from school saying, "Hair like Jehwee's." At first I had no idea what he was talking about and called Jeff's mother and asked if Jeff had changed his hair style.

The most awful haircut experiences up to this point had included the electronic clippers. We would warn the hairdressers if they even pulled them out of the drawer that they were going to lose their tip. And here was a haircut that *only* involved electronic clippers.

But, oh, the peer pressure. Sean wanted that haircut—bad. After a month of him begging every day, "Hair like Jehwee," I told him I would take him, but he had to sit in the chair by himself, and if he even tried one time to bat the hairstylist's hand away, the cut would stop immediately. I also told him I would take him to McDonald's and let him play in the balls and tunnels if he would sit still.

He hopped up into the swiveling chair, the hairdresser Velcro'd the smock around his neck, and he was struggling to sit still. She pulled out the clippers and began the buzz cut. I sat nearby in the waiting area pretending to read a magazine, waiting for him to reach up and swat the clippers away. He wanted that haircut—bad. He didn't take his eyes off the mirror. He made faces, but he sat still, and he clasped his hands in his lap, struggling to not take a swipe at the stylist. And he got it—the buzz cut! Afterward, he couldn't stop rubbing his head and pointed and told everybody, "Hair like Jehwee." From that day onward, Sean was great for haircuts, and by the time he was 10, we could give him the money, he would walk in, give his name to let them know he was there, pay and tip the stylist, and I would really read a magazine in the waiting area. Positive Peer Pressure—Success!

Reading with a Purpose

Discovery consists of looking at the same thing as everyone else and thinking something different. — Roger von Oech

We moved into a new house when Sean was in first grade. To help Sean read, we typed out labels and glued them to 3x5 notecards and taped them onto all of the furniture, on the doors, on everything so he could learn to sight-read the names of each household item. I didn't realize how well he was reading.

Sean was situated in front of the TV watching the best babysitter ever . . . Barney the Purple Dinosaur. I was just stepping into the shower when I smelled it. The unmistakable odor of microwave popcorn being popped—and I anticipated the next odor to be the unmistakable odor of *burnt* microwave popcorn. It was a winter day and too cold to open the windows to air out the house—and I didn't want to bring the ladder into the house to turn off the smoke detectors—so I threw on my robe and ran downstairs to stop the popcorn before the inevitable burning was to occur.

As I entered the kitchen, Sean was sitting on the counter, his feet on the chair he had pushed over to climb up onto the countertop. He was opening the door of the vent-mounted microwave, carefully avoiding the burners on the oven below, and removing a perfectly popped bag of popcorn. I stopped, amazed, because I could never get the microwave to make such a perfectly popped bag of popcorn. I always scorched a few kernels in each bag. I asked Sean, "How many minutes did you pop that for?"

He looked at me like I was crazy. I reworded my question, "What numbers did you push?"

Again, the confused look, then he pointed to the control panel of the microwave and said, "Popcorn."

Duh! We had lived there about a month, and I didn't know there was a "popcorn" button on the microwave. *I* was the slow learner. Sean was using his newly acquired reading ability to make himself a snack he knew I wouldn't have allowed at 8 a.m.

Indian Guides

There are two ways to live your life. One is as though nothing is a miracle, the other is as though everything is a miracle. —Albert Einstein

Today they are called Y Guides because it was deemed inappropriate to call them Indian Guides and Indian Princesses. We expect people to be respectful of our kids with disabilities, so we respect the decision to change the name of the club.

Sean and Rick joined the YMCA Indian Guides when Sean was in special education kindergarten. I loved that they went camping one weekend every month. It was a great break for me, and it was great bonding time for Sean and Rick. Inclusion in an Indian Guide Tribe was easy. It was too bad Sean was the only person with any disability in their tribe.

Rick became friends with the group of dads he would later serve with on the Little League Baseball and Pop Warner Football boards. The club only lasts from kindergarten through third grade, and the last year Rick was the chief of Sean's tribe. Rick and Sean both got to wear the headdresses too. (That was the last year they had headdresses. They ceremoniously buried them when the name changed to Y Guides.) Sean's Indian Guide name was Running Smile, and Rick was Smiling Bull. During their weekly meetings they sat in a circle and passed around the "Talking Stick." Each member of the tribe had to tell about something that had happened at school that week. Sean learned to take turns and to only talk when he was holding the talking stick. Lessons of turn taking and knowing when to talk and when not to are important in many areas of our lives other than just in school.

There was a FASCAR Derby each year, and Rick would work and work on making a fast and cool car from that block of wood. Sean ended up with a couple of trophies from Dad's speedy creations.

Participating in Indian Guides with other boys from Sean's regular education classes was a big relationship builder. One boy became really good friends with Sean. Rick and I became good friends with his parents as well. One camping trip they went to was on Catalina Island. Rick woke up early one morning to this boy alerting him that Sean had left their three-sided tent. He was trying to be quiet and not wake anybody else up, but kept repeating, "Emergency—Sean. Emergency—Sean." Rick went to see what was going on, and there Sean was, by himself, in his red-footy-pajamas, sitting on the wet sand on the beach throwing rocks into the water. Sean felt safe and confident enough to strike out on his own, and his friends were watching out for him, even if Dad was still sleeping.

The Indian Guide camps exposed Sean to a lot of "guy" stuff. They shot a .22 rifle and in archery shot bows and arrows, learned to camp . . . when I asked Rick—a man of few words—what else they did he said, "That's about it." I am sure there's more, but you're going to have to ask a guy who talks more.

Organizations, clubs, and sports that allow people to build relationships with common interests and activities outside of school further solidify friendships in school.

Cub Scouts

Following the Scout law sounds like a game plan that would give us all a better chance for success in life—and I mean every area of life. —Zig Ziglar

After Sean graduated from Indian Guides he joined the Cub Scout chapter at his elementary school. He liked the activities, the hikes, and the FASCAR Derby races. I don't have a lot of stories. Cub Scouts happened after school, and I never had to drive him or volunteer for anything, so I wasn't there. That was nice. Sean's future fifth-grade teacher was his Den Mother, and that was a benefit when he got to fifth grade because they already knew each other, and he skipped his typical testing period at the beginning of school.

He attended weekly meetings without an aide or any help. His troop was made up of eight boys, all in the third grade. He used appropriate peer skills most of the time, and his peers helped to remind him of appropriate behavior.

He loved playing games, being in skits, practicing skills like knot tying, first aid, and wood working, hiking and fitness. When I asked his Den Mother if he actually tied the knots, she told me that one of the other boys would put the rope into a loop to help him get started, then he would finish it. She also told me they learned to throw a rescue rope, in case somebody was in the water, and he loved throwing the rope to the target.

Sean earned many belt loops because he was involved with so

many activities and sports. Each month there was a Den Meeting and his Den Mother would award each Cub Scout with the belt loops they had earned for the month. Sean was thrilled when he got to go on stage and be presented with his belt loops. He made the decision that he didn't want to move on to Boy Scouts in sixth grade because he preferred sports to scouting, but many young men with Down syndrome earn their Eagle Scout Award.

Communication

When you don't talk, there's a lot of stuff that ends up not getting said.
—Catherine Gilbert Murdock

Independence is almost impossible if you can't communicate in some form. We were not sure whether Sean would ever talk intelligibly and started using American Sign Language when he was a baby. By the time he was 1 year old he knew about 50 signs. If he was eating something he really liked he would get excited and sign every sign that he knew to make sure you knew he wanted: "More, Please, Now, Eat."

Augmentative Communication Devices in the '90s were very large and extremely expensive and really not a viable option for us at that point. But today, an iPhone, iPad, or iPod Touch works great as long as the person can type or touch photos or even simply look at images that will talk for them. (If iPads existed when he was that young we would have had a Picture Exchange Communication System PECS on it.)

Sean was born with his right ear canal collapsed. A hearing test at 2 months old showed he had very little function of his right ear, and thankfully, normal hearing in his left ear. At age 3, he qualified for a grant to receive one hearing aid and wore it until first grade. He was retested yearly and in a subsequent hearing test it was determined the hearing aid wasn't any benefit. The hearing had deteriorated so much he couldn't hear a jet if he was standing behind it on the runway. He has learned to make sure that he is sitting with his left ear toward anybody speaking and has no problem telling people he is deaf in his right ear and can't hear them if there is a lot of background noise.

When Sean was 3 years old in Washington State the Medicaid Deeming allowed for private speech therapy in addition to what he received at school. He had this wonderful speech and language pathologist who was able to do some great assessments. She diagnosed him with Oral Motor Apraxia and a Phonological Processing Disorder due to his hearing loss. The recommendation was for speech therapy 5 days a week, 30 minutes a day.

Oral Motor Apraxia means that he couldn't imitate the shape of her mouth when she showed him how to form his lips and tongue to create sounds. The information is in his brain, but it can't get from his brain to his lips. (Ever have a name on the "tip of your tongue"? That's Apraxia.)

Phonological Processing Disorder means because he was deaf in one ear he didn't "hear" sounds the same as everyone else. Sean also had a narrow palate which crowded his mouth and made it more difficult to create sounds. Compounded all together you would think he never would talk— but he wouldn't shut up. (He may have inherited that trait from me.) We just couldn't understand what he was saying. He was still signing so that helped a ton so we could understand what he was communicating by him showing us.

At age 3, Sean started having an opinion about what he wanted to eat for breakfast, lunch, and dinner. I had always made what I wanted to for dinner, and he ate what I put in front of him. But now he was mentally deciding what he wanted to eat, and if I put something in front of him that was different than what he thought he wanted, he would have a *terrible threes* crying fit.

We finally had to photograph the food that he liked prepared and made a photo menu so Sean could point and order his meals to limit the amount of meltdowns related to mealtime. If I was out of a certain item I would cover it with a Post-it Note.

The daily speech therapy made a huge difference in his receptive language, but not his articulation. The recommendation the speech therapist made was that he have a palate expander put in as soon as possible to help him make sounds more clearly. We decided to wait until we moved back to California since we were certain that we had a long road of orthodontia ahead of us.

After we moved I decided to call Children's Hospital for a referral, and they recommended an orthodontist who was a part of their cranial-facial clinic. I mistakenly thought he would have experience with children with intellectual disabilities.

One thing to know is that customarily the first appointment with an orthodontist is free. Sean had some major oral motor defensiveness. He didn't like anybody in his mouth. Dentist visits had consisted of me lying on him, holding his body down while a dental assistant held his hands and the dentist or hygienist QUICKLY cleaned his teeth. By age 5 when we saw the first orthodontist we had experienced 6 cleanings that were always a *ton of fun*. I warned the doctor that Sean wasn't going to cooperate, and I made the wrong assumption that since he was recommended by Children's Hospital, and saw children with cranial-facial issues, he would be prepared . . . or at least tolerant.

Sean happily jumped into the exam chair and closed his lips tight. I tried to explain to him that the doctor was just "looking," and he wasn't going to do anything to him. But he fought and pulled out all the stops. The doctor was finally able to get a peek at his high narrow palate. Then he looked at me with a sad face and said, "Yes, he has a high palate, and he could benefit from a palate expander, but really, is the trauma worth it? Why bother?"

WHY BOTHER? Wow . . . well . . . So he could speak more clearly . . . So he could have a future of good oral hygiene and health. So he could look attractive. I was fuming.

I had a friend who was looking into an orthodontist for her daughter who also has Down syndrome, and she found one who had done her doctoral thesis on Down syndrome. So, I scheduled an appointment with her. She was understanding, patient, and got into Sean's mouth. Her recommendation was that his teeth weren't ready yet, and she had me come back every 6 months—free of charge—to track his progress and growth. When Sean was 8, she sent him for photos and X-rays. The next step was to make a plaster impression of his upper jaw. She had an exam room with a door that closed in her office. I hope it was soundproof, because Sean sounded like somebody was tearing him limb from limb. I lay on him, and there were TWO assistants, one holding each arm and a third holding his head still. This amazing orthodontist got the impression of Sean's upper jaw in only two tries.

One week later we returned to begin the process of installing the palate expander. Sean was a little better, but still fought while she put the bands on his teeth. We returned the next day for the expander to be added. Each time he was better than the time before. We also started using an electric toothbrush (Dad held him down, I brushed) and that helped build his tolerance for oral activity.

Every night for 30 days I had to put in a little key in the expander and make one turn. In 30 days, Sean's palate was widened to its goal width. Sean was gradually allowing us into his mouth without a fight, and his articulation made exponential improvements with a wider palate. Sean visited the orthodontist every month, and within 6 months, he would get into the exam chair by himself and sit without being held down anymore. Progress—no matter how slow, is still progress.

One year after getting the palate expander he had braces put on his teeth. At first, his speech got worse, but then with all that metal in his mouth to keep his tongue busy working over the appliance over and over again his speech improved and his oral motor strength and coordination continued to improve.

By the time he was in fifth grade, his speech was intelligible to most people, and he was having actual conversations.

Sean ended up needing braces three times. The third time because he wouldn't wear the top retainer after the second set. His palate began to collapse, and his orthodontist jumped right in with another set of braces. After that round she installed a permanent palate expander, and he has a beautiful smile.

To answer the first orthodontist's question: *Why bother?*—Because—IT WAS WORTH IT.

(NOTE: Palate expanders must be in place before the maxillary bones are fused. After that, it is too late for an expander. Most orthodontists will see patients the first time (around age 6) at no charge in order to determine the right time to begin oral appliances.)

Eyeglasses

I was walking down the street wearing glasses when the prescription ran out.—Steven Wright

The ophthalmologist made 5-year-old-Sean and I wait in his tiny claustrophobic exam room for an hour. I was at my wit's end trying to keep him from playing with and subsequently damaging the motorized chair, the movable light, and all the other gadgets that I am sure cost thousands of dollars. (Which I could not begin to pay for if Sean damaged them.) I tried to entertain Sean with the boring magazines stored in a rack on the wall by having him walk over to the rack, retrieve a magazine, then we, page-by-page, looked at all the pictures. He would return the magazine to the rack and retrieve another one. Finally, Eye Doctor graced us with his presence.

Sean got up and returned the current magazine to the rack on the wall. The doctor was astounded. It was as if Sean had stood up and recited the Magna Carta. He turned to me and said, "I've read where *these children* grow up and love to do tedious, repetitive tasks that would bore you and me. I think he has a great future with performing repetitive tasks." I should have decided that would be our last appointment with this doctor if the most he expected my son to do in the future were tedious, repetitive tasks, which would have been great, because Sean considered writing his letters and numbers as a tedious, repetitive task at that point and truly hated to do that. But instead of changing doctors we kept going to him.

On a subsequent annual vision exam Sean was in the beginning of third grade and was reading pretty well. He was still having a hard time writing with his fine motor issues. At the end of that exam the ophthalmologist said, "Well, he's still farsighted."

I wasn't sure I had heard him, "Still? Still farsighted? You have never said he was farsighted before. Shouldn't we have a prescription for glasses?"

The doctor gave me a confused look and said, "I don't think you need to go to the trouble and expense of getting eyeglasses. It's not like he's ever going to read."

I went off on him. "Sean is already reading. It's not your place to limit my son's progress based on outdated, prejudicial opinions. And it isn't your place to decide whether we can afford eyeglasses or not. Please write the prescription for the glasses right this minute."

Yet another doctor we never saw again. I asked around, and my friends referred me to a great ophthalmologist that Sean still sees today. Sadly, I have heard this story from other parents about other ophthalmologists as well.

Over the years, Sean has had a love-hate relationship with his glasses. They are a fashion statement to him. All it takes is one girl to make a negative comment about his glasses and he stops wearing them. As an adult, he has refused to wear anything but prescription sunglasses. He doesn't seem to have a problem reading texts on his iPhone, and he can see to play his video games and read menus, so we haven't made a big deal about him not wearing them. Many adults don't wear their glasses like they should.

The Disability Discount

Our prime purpose in this life is to help others. And if you can't help them, at least don't hurt them. —Dalai Lama

Sean is a master manipulator and has been from the beginning of his life. He has an uncanny sense of people's feelings and can read people and play them. In school, he would act like he couldn't do something in order to get somebody else to do it for him. I had to watch carefully each year at school for the girls with the maternal instincts and make sure they didn't baby Sean into being a baby. But when he was around sixth grade, I realized he also had a way of manipulating strangers.

One day after school, Sean accompanied me to a store where I needed to get my cell phone replaced. He was thirsty, and there was a fast-food restaurant next door. I gave him $2 and told him to get a medium soda, then come back. A few minutes later he returned with a *giant* soda that would have cost over $3. After I was done at the cell phone store, I took Sean to the fast-food restaurant and apologized to the man behind the counter and offered to pay the rest of the amount for the soda.

"No worries, I just gave him the soda. It's all right."

"No, it's not all right. Sean needs to pay for drinks, just like every-body else. If he thinks sodas are free, then he's going to expect free sodas everywhere."

The man still refused to take my money. And Sean did learn that lesson well.

We experienced discounts when we took Sean and his friends with disabilities bowling. The lane would be $15 an hour for anybody else, and they only charged our boys $6. He would get entrance to events free. It was embarrassing how often he would receive free items.

It was as though the people giving him free things were granting themselves some sort of sainthood. So we began calling it the *disability discount* whenever Sean got a break. I tell this story because many of the upcoming stories include moments of disability discounts.

Benefits of Physical Fitness and Sports

I've missed more than 9,000 shots in my career. I've lost almost 300 games. 26 times, I've been trusted to take the game-winning shot and missed. I've failed over and over again in my life. And that is why I succeed.—Michael Jordan

We all know that getting off the couch is good for us. But for people with Down syndrome and other disabilities it could make a huge difference in their independence and their cognition. A small pilot study of adolescents with Down syndrome who exercised on a stationary bicycle revealed that it improved their speed of information processing and manual dexterity, even after only one Assisted Cycle Therapy session. In 2013, Shannon D. R. Ringenbach, an associate professor of kinesiology in the School of Nutrition and Health Promotion at Arizona State University, received a grant from the Eunice Shriver National Institute of Child Health and Human Development to conduct a longer term study.

The great thing about Challenger Sports—sport teams for youth with disabilities—is you don't have to be good at the sport. It's the participation and the physical activity that benefits all people with any disability

Being on a team provides social skills you can't get anywhere else. Taking direction from a coach is important in future job situations and helps in school as well. Sean would listen to a coach before he would listen to me—that included when Dad was the coach—he listened better than at home. Performing your role on the team helps build confidence and is a start to performing independently. Practice, waiting your turn, patience and persistence are learned. And you have to practice for everything you do in school, practice writing, practice reading, so understanding that practice is a part of life is learned in sports. Patience is learned when you are in the dugout, on the sidelines, or waiting for the ball to come in your direction. Persistence is the biggest benefit. If our kids give up, they will never achieve anything. Sean is the most persistent person I know, and he negotiates skillfully for things he wants to do or items he wants to buy. The ability to never give up is important to all of us.

Sports

All people, regardless of whether they're athletes or not, should treat people the way they want to be treated. —Walter Payton

I have never been very athletic. But I married a man who was a jock in high school, playing football, baseball, and he wrestled. I met Rick when he was in his early 30s and had a perpetually sore shoulder from his baseball career. It was a given that he would be coaching Sean's sports teams.

When Sean was a baby he struggled to roll over, sit up, and crawl. But once he started walking it took no time for him to start to run. Sean was 2½ when I enrolled us in a Mommy and Me Gymnastics class, and he continued gymnastics until he was 6. I have always struggled with my weight, and I believed that by building his muscles with the various exercises that increased his muscle tone that this set him up for loving physical activity for life. Sean also inherited his father's athletic ability. He was coordinated and could hit a pitched ball at only 4 years old.

When we moved into our new house we found an 8 foot round trampoline that was only 2 feet off the ground. This was before the ones that have safety nets around them existed. The good thing about the small size was the kids had to take turns jumping one at a time, so that minimized injuries as well.

We had Santa deliver the trampoline, and on Christmas morning we were in the middle of opening presents, when Sean suddenly stopped dead in his tracks—he had seen the trampoline through the window. He didn't say a word but dropped the present he had in his hands and took off running toward the patio door, slid the door open, and the rest of the gifts had to wait an hour or so. We could not get him off of that trampoline.

Sean has a very toned body. He has 6-pack abs, and I believe the trampoline made the difference in his balance, his core strength, and overall great physical condition at an early age.

Baseball

In the spring of his special education kindergarten year we signed Sean up for Challenger Baseball through the Little League. Rick began as an assistant coach on his team, later coaching a team, then becoming the commissioner of the Challenger Division.

Sean had been throwing things his whole life so he was able to throw the baseball pretty accurately at 5 years old. Even though Sean could hit a pitched ball, the Challenger Juniors batted off of a tee, so Sean did too. His first at bat, he smashed the ball down the middle toward the pitcher, and promptly ran to third base.

The regular Little League provided their 12 year olds—who played in the Major's division teams—as buddies to be paired with the Junior Challengers to teach them the game of baseball one-on-one. Those boys didn't know anything about disabilities, but they knew about the game of baseball and what being a friend was.

As Sean did with every new teacher, he would test his buddy— and every week he had a new one—so the game of throwing his glove over the outfield fence and making his buddy climb over and get it for him ensued every weekend. I finally had to warn the buddies in advance not to retrieve it, and if they did, not to give it back to Sean—he had figured out how to command and boss them around without saying a word. He would laugh hysterically when they would chase his glove over the fence, and as soon as they gave it back to him he would throw it over the fence again.

Over the next 13 years, Sean learned the game of baseball well.

He even tried out at his elementary school and made the sixth-grade team for the traditional softball game of the sixth graders vs. the teachers. Only 18 out of 150 students made the team, and he truly qualified for the position.

In high school, Sean was placed as the Varsity Baseball Team's assistant. He knew the game and was a great encourager for the team. They fed off of his love for the game.

During his last year of Challenger Baseball, he was hitting home runs over the fence. After he graduated from high school, Sean became an assistant coach for a Challenger Team. And he has a goal of working at Angel Stadium as an usher. Baseball is definitely a passion learned early.

Soccer

We learned about AYSO Soccer sign-ups through our regular education friends, and signed Sean up to play when he was turning 6, during his regular education kindergarten year. I stood in line with hundreds of parents waiting to sign their children up—then I saw the sign—"Volunteers needed, Coaches and Referees sign up here." There was nobody in that line, so I signed Rick up to be a referee. He wasn't happy with me. He had never played soccer and didn't really know the rules. But after one clinic that the league provided he was up to speed and ready for his duty each week.

Sean's first 3 years in soccer he was on regular teams, and there was another player who had autism on his team. This was true inclusion. At this age, soccer has no real rules, no real form—both teams of players simply chased the ball wherever it rolled. It looked more like a swarm of bees than a team with positions. Sean further learned to listen and follow directions, and he was on a team with kids he would be in regular education with for many years to come. When they started keeping score we transitioned him to an AYSO VIP Soccer team for kids with disabilities. Rick was the assistant coach with the same man who was Sean's baseball coach.

Basketball

Because regular AYSO Soccer was so accepting, we signed Sean up for our Community Basketball League. The format of each session was to practice for the first half hour, then play a game the second half hour. Nobody loses; everybody wins. At 6 years old, Sean really struggled. Even though they had lowered the goal to 8 feet, Sean could not even hit the bottom of the net with the ball. For 8 weeks he tried and tried to just get the ball high enough to reach the goal, much less make a basket. But he never got discouraged, he never gave up. At the last practice he finally made ONE basket. All of his teammates gave him high fives over and over again. The parents clapped and cheered; the coach put him up on his shoulders and paraded him around the court. Sean was hooked on basketball. For Christmas that year we bought him a basketball hoop for our driveway. He practiced and practiced, and today, he can hit three-pointers with nothing but net.

A couple of great parents started a league for teens and adults with disabilities, and Sean played and learned to pass the ball and how to strategize on the court. It was great exercise to run up and down the court, and great spatial awareness to maneuver around people without mowing them down.

Swimming

The first summer of Sean's life we signed up for a Mommy and Me swimming class through the YMCA. In a heated pool, Sean learned to hold his breath and to roll onto his back when in the water. Sean loved the water. He still does. Sean began swimming lessons at a local swim school when he was 2, and from watching the other children in his class, and the assistance of his instructor, he learned to kick, and he learned to move his arms. But it wasn't until he was 6 years old that he was able to both kick and use his arms at the same time.

Swimming opened so many more sports to Sean. When he was a teen we went to Hawaii for the first time, and Sean learned to snorkel. When he swam into water too deep to stand up he would panic. So we rented him a Boogie Board so he would have something to hold onto and that boosted his confidence in the deeper waters. Modifications and adaptations are available in every area of life.

Kayaking, sailing stand-up, and paddle-boarding are all sports that Sean has enjoyed because he is able to swim and is comfortable in the water.

Surfing

When Sean was in fifth grade he asked me if he could learn to surf. I didn't know anybody who surfed, so I just forgot about it. Each summer he asked me again, and finally in the spring before ninth grade, I learned about an inclusive surf school in Seal Beach—M&M Surf School. I signed Sean up, and then told him he was going to finally learn to surf.

"I don't want to learn to surf anymore."

"What? You've been asking me for 3 years, why not?"

"I just don't."

Since I had already signed him up I called the surf camp instructor, Michael, and explained that I needed to remove Sean's enrollment from camp. Michael knew what had happened. He said, "Once they get to a certain age, they think it will be too hard. Bring him for a private lesson, and I will get him standing his first time out, then he'll want to come to camp."

Rick and I drove Sean to Seal Beach one Saturday and met with Michael the Surfer Dude. A great guy in his late 40s who took to Sean immediately. He walked Sean to the shoreline and worked with him on lying on the board, then showed him how to stand up while they were still on the sand. He had a long board—really, it was as big as a sidewalk. That was the size of board I had learned to surf on (the one time I surfed) when I first moved to California.

Sure enough, he got Sean to stand up on his first wave on the board. Sean went to surf camp for a week and because I couldn't pick him up at noon I also signed him up for a corresponding afternoon marine biology camp where they put on masks and snorkels and discovered what was under the water from the decks of their surf-boards. When I picked Sean up each day at 3:00 he was asleep before we left the parking lot and barely woke up for dinner. That was a quiet week at our house. We repeated this camp a couple of more summers when Sean had a free week and needed something fun to do.

Snow Skiing

We had Sean try everything that was available, but he didn't love every sport. I love living in warm Southern California, but less than 3 hours away you can drive up to Big Bear Mountain and snow ski in the winter.

We learned about the USARC—United States Adaptive Recreation Center—and called to schedule a ski lesson for Sean. They have amazing volunteers who will ski with people with disabilities for a half day or a full day, teaching them to snow ski or simply accompanying them on the slopes if they are independent. For people in wheelchairs, they have ski chairs that the volunteers maneuver—one of our friends did this and loved it.

Sean is a lot like me. He doesn't like the cold . . . He didn't like the heavy ski boots and all of the hats, scarves, and gloves. He skied three different times, but disliked it so much we never returned. I think if we had gone for a few days in a row it would have been different, but driving up for a half-day lesson three times, and with a whole year in between lessons didn't give him the exposure he needed to get and stay interested. But many of his friends do love to snow ski.

Volleyball

Sean also played volleyball in the Community Recreation League. He learned the rules of the game. Volleyball also was mostly girls, and that was a big motivator for Sean as well. We only signed him up a couple of times because our schedule was pretty full. He learned enough that he is able to play for fun and on vacations he rules the pool when there is a water volleyball net and is very comfortable in a game of beach volleyball too.

Bowling

When Sean was very young, our Regional Center (Department of Developmental Disabilities) newsletter had a sort of personal ad section where adults with disabilities could post their interests so they could meet up with others who shared their interests to form friendships. One of my friends whose son was in Sean's Early Intervention program pointed out to me one day that everyone in those ads said they liked to bowl. We joked for years that bowling must be a requisite sport for people with disabilities. Then when one ambitious mom decided that there wasn't enough for our kids to do during the summers she started a bowling league. Sean bowled with them the first year she started the league—he was 7 years old. He could barely pick up the lightest bowling ball. As he grew up we found his fingers were too big for the 10 pound balls that they had for use at the bowling alley so for Christmas when he was 15 we bought him a bowling ball.

He loved seeing them drill the custom finger holes into his 8.5 pound ball. He learned to properly throw the ball once his fingers fit into the holes, but he banked it off the bumpers, never letting us get a lane without bumpers. He later took bowling at the community college where they taught him how to play without bumpers. To date, the best game he has bowled is 170, and he cheers himself and anyone else who can score a strike.

Golf

Sean began Special Olympics Golf at 8 years old. Some friends of ours provided him some little golf clubs that their daughter had grown out of. Our local golf course hosted the practices and provided a nine-hole tournament at the end of the season. Two golf pros from the course and another volunteer split the 40 athletes into three groups, rotating them between putting, chipping, and driving. Each week the 1½ hour practices were further supported by volunteers from the local Catholic high school golf team. There were so many volunteers it was usually two Special Olympics golfers to one high school golf team member. Sean learned the game well, and just like his dad, became addicted. No matter what sport he was currently playing we would ask him what his favorite sport was, and the answer was always "Golf."

At the end of the 6 weeks of practice the course hosted an Alternating Shot tournament. Alternating shot is where one golfer tees off, then their partner hits the ball wherever it lies and so on. Each Special Olympics golfer had a volunteer partner, and the course provided carts for the volunteers to drive. It was not a sanctioned Special Olympics tournament—in a Special Olympics-sanctioned tournament the golfers are required to walk the nine-hole course. Rick was Sean's partner until he had a surgery one year, so we had to ask for a volunteer to play with Sean.

Sean was 11 years old and somehow was able to hit the ball straight, a skill I have never mastered. He didn't have a lot of distance on the ball. He was averaging around 15 yards for each drive, but hitting it straight was amazing.

Sean's volunteer was a newly retired woman who was married to a scratch golfer. She was learning the game so she could play golf with her husband in their retirement. Her husband was in their foursome with another Special Olympian who has autism and is nonverbal. His Special Olympics partner also hit the ball with the same force whether he was 2 inches from the cup or driving off the tee.

Sean teed off on the first hole and whacked it perfectly down the center of the fairway. His volunteer immediately began apologizing. "Oh, Sean, I am so sorry. I am not anywhere near as good as you are." And she wasn't. As she attempted to hit the ball where it lay, she topped it and it dribbled off to the right about 10 feet. Sean was very gracious and forgiving at 11 years old. He spent the rest of the nine holes encouraging her, "It's OK, you'll do better next time."

Rick is no longer able to play golf, so now when Sean has a volunteer partner we have to ask that the person can play golf decently. His most recent partner, who was a duffer, wasn't treated as kindly as the first one. Sean just looked at the guy and said, "You suck." Thankfully, his volunteer had a sense of humor and agreed with him.

After playing nine holes of golf, the Special Olympians and their volunteer partners congregate outside the club house for pizza—which the pros purchase out of their own pockets—and there is a medal ceremony. The head pro always makes it very entertaining. He creates categories based on current successful golfers' names, and each athlete and their partner ends up with either a bronze, silver, or gold medal.

Rick and I tried to calculate the cost of the golf course and the pros once. The Special Olympians take up an entire practice green and half of the driving range at a prime time on Saturday. They provide the balls free for the Special Olympians to putt, chip, and drive. The tournament itself is a huge cost with half a round of golf, including cart, on a Saturday—and there are 80 people playing in the tournament. Then the two pros donate an hour and a half of their time, for 6 to 8 weeks, when they could be giving golf lessons for a fee. Special Olympics provides a minimal fee to the course. We calculated the course's commitment to be over $20,000 per season.

The golf course, the same two pros, and the Catholic high school golf team continues to support the program—now in its twelfth year.

When Sean went to community college, both his first and second semesters he took Golf and earned A's in the classes.

Rick's company has a golf tournament every spring. Rick can only chip and putt now, but he takes Sean to be in his foursome at his company tournament. It's a scramble (everybody takes a shot, and they use the ball lying in the best place for the next shot), and they use Sean's balls quite a bit during the tournament. Their team has won a few times, and come home with the trophy.

Sean's skill in golf has allowed him to perform the Ceremonial First Drive for the Down Syndrome Association of Orange County's Annual Fundraising Golf Tournament. Today, golf is still his favorite sport.

Life after Bike Camp

Life is like riding a bicycle: you don't fall off unless you stop pedaling.
—Claude Pepper

Sean is extremely athletic. He's coordinated. While he has major fine motor issues and hates to write, he excels in gross motor exercises. He can hit a pitched ball, throw, and catch. He can kick accurately. He can sink baskets over and over again. He's always had a great tenacity to stick with something he wants to stick with until he learns it. But riding a bike was not one of those things. We had tried tricycles, training wheels, trailer bikes, but nothing gave him the confidence to overcome his fears of falling off the bike. Riding a bike requires not only coordination, but confidence. Pedaling, steering, balancing, and watching where you are going. That is a lot to coordinate and do all at one time.

Sean attended the *Lose the Training Wheels Bike Camp* between his freshman and sophomore years. The inventor of this camp saw the possibilities and set out to devise a way to teach children, teens, and adults with disabilities how to ride a two-wheel bike. People like him are my heroes—instead of seeing the impossibilities, they see what is possible, then make it a reality. He engineered wheels that can be interchanged off of a bike that look like rolling pins of different sizes. On this bike the students gain confidence when they don't fall and achieve success in riding around and around and around the indoor arena. Utilizing volunteer assistants to run beside the bikes to provide more confidence and encouragement—the results are spectacular. The wheels are changed as the student progresses, and the degree of difficulty increases over the week. They provide guidelines for the parents on types of bicycles to purchase, and by the end of the week, the student is riding his or her very own bicycle.

Sean started off with the wide rear wheels that look like giant rolling pins progressing quickly through the eight different sizes. He had a little distraction on the second day when a girl he had a huge crush on made it off the waiting list and joined the class, but he soon recovered from his lovesickness when she moved past his ability level—the competitive part of him set in.

He had two helpers who were high school athletes, and he thought it was funny when he rode faster and faster and they had to run faster and faster to keep up with him.

By Wednesday afternoon, armed with the set of recommendations for an appropriate bike provided by the camp we went to the store and purchased Sean a new bike, with a few custom features, including a wide seat. By Thursday, he was on his very own new two-wheel bike. The final class on Friday consisted of practicing starting and using the brakes to stop. A nice medal and certificate was presented at the end.

And then we came home. When Rick got home from work Sean jumped on his bike to show Dad what he could do. Sean told me I needed to give him a push to get started. He rode a few feet, then skidded to a stop before making the first turn—I gave him another push, and he rode around our cul-de-sac once, twice, then was finished.

Now, Sean isn't the kind of kid who will say, "I'm scared," and he won't cry. But when he is scared or nervous or has any sort of anxiety he yells and acts angry. On Saturday, I broke my bike out of the mothballs—and tried to ride with him. I noticed that he kept looking down at his feet on the pedals, then he would realize he wasn't watching where he was going and get spooked, and then would skid to a stop. Then he couldn't even get started because he wouldn't look up. I felt like we had gone backward and was afraid the money I had spent on the class and the new bike were going to be a waste—but we kept going—every day riding for a few minutes . . . a few minutes more—then 2 weeks later it was time to venture out.

Sean loves Taco Bell, and there is one four blocks from our house. I didn't let him have Taco Bell for a week, so he was experiencing serious bean-burrito withdrawals. We also live near a lake which has a very wide sidewalk around it. Sean's mission was to ride once around the 1-mile-lake's path, then we would walk our bikes to Taco Bell from there—and he did it. With his confidence growing we decided to give the beach a try.

I put a new bike rack on my car, and Rick, Sean, and I drove to Huntington Beach. I decided to start at a parking lot that is 3 miles from the pier. The wide sidewalk wasn't crowded this day. Rick was sure that 3 miles was too far, but I was determined to get some distance on Sean's bike. He started off a little wobbly, then pedaled really fast. Then after about 5 minutes he declared that he was finished riding. We were nowhere near the pier yet. I explained to him that we were going to a restaurant at the pier, THEN we were going to have ice cream, but if he couldn't make it, then we'd just go home.

He could see the pier, so the visual goal was set. He also wanted that ice cream, so he mustered up the energy to go a little further—all the while Rick was giving me the *"I told you so"* look. Sean did make it the whole 3 miles to the pier and was very proud of his accomplishment. We ate lunch, he had his ice cream, then we hopped back on the bikes to ride back to the car.

Rick wanted to be sure Sean made it back to the car, so he created a little competition and told me to hang back so they could ride ahead and beat me to the car, so I stayed back. I was enjoying riding my bike again after so many years. There was a time when I lived near the beach that I would ride my bike everywhere.

As I rode along I came upon a bike down in the middle of the path—it was Sean. OH NO, he crashed. And being the drama king that he is was showing everybody the blood dripping from his knee. I asked Rick what happened—he rear-ended a walking teenage girl. She was wearing a bikini, so that may have been the reason he ran into her. Well, the best part? He got right back on that bike and headed out so he could still beat me to the car.

We were almost back to the car when the walkway got crowded again . . . and to avoid hitting another person Sean rode off the pathway into the sand. The bike stopped dead, but Sean didn't—he did a complete header over the handlebars. Thank God for that helmet. He skinned his shoulder up, and reinjured his skinned knees, but got up laughing and got back on the bike, and we finally made it to the car.

Now Sean can ride, likes to ride, and recovers from crashes. He rode 6 miles that day, and it was the beginning of embarking upon many journeys on our bikes.

Karate

We tried karate with Sean's friends from his first-grade class . . . until one day he kicked his first-grade teacher. I had picked him up after school and she told me earlier that day she was trying to get him to do some writing, and he had kicked her. This was a new behavior for Sean, and as I drove him to his karate class's yellow-belt test, I racked my brain as to where he would have learned to kick.

As I sat watching his karate test it dawned on me—karate—he was learning to kick in karate. I asked his teacher the next morning if he had said anything when he kicked her.

"It sounded like 'yee-ha,'" she responded.

I groaned, "Oh, *kiai*. Great, that's what they say when they punch and kick in karate." We decided he needed to wait until he was able to understand *when* it was appropriate to use karate, and kicking his teacher to avoid writing wasn't really appropriate.

Sean was in seventh grade and 13 years old when our Down Syndrome Association hosted a weekly karate class. The Sensei reinforced constantly that you only use karate if you are in danger. If Sean had any behaviors that were inappropriate in school we would tell Sensei, and he would have Sean do sit-ups or push-ups as a consequence. Sean respected Sensei and listened to him.

When he was teaching sparring, Sensei would spar with his students to show them what to do, and he wouldn't punch or kick them hard. During Sean's first sparring session he wasn't very appropriate. They were in a stance with their hands up like boxers. Sean gestured with his hand, waving his fingers as if to say, "Bring it." Rick and Sensei were doing their best not to die laughing as Sensei took Sean down to the ground over and over. Finally he explained to Sean to stop the taunt because that was why he was taking him down.

When Sean was 19 he earned his black belt. Sean was getting

close to moving into his supported independent living apartment, and we were winding down all of his activities. I was satisfied with his fourth-degree brown belt, but Sean was determined to earn that black belt. He practiced the 50-Step Kata at home between classes, watching a video of Sensei going through the steps.

The black belt test was more challenging than anything Sean had ever done. He had to spar with TWO black belts—both had been his Senseis. They didn't make it easy and kicked his butt. I almost stopped the test, but then Sean finally scored his points. The 2-hour test was grueling, and Sean has every reason to be very proud of that black belt he earned.

Flag Football

When Sean was starting high school, the National Pop Warner Football League started a Challenger Flag Football division. They also started Challenger Cheerleading too. Rick got involved with football immediately and helped to start it locally and coached Sean's team. Sean loves football. He threw a natural spiral the first time he ever threw a football. He could catch passes, but there was only one other player on their team who could also pass and catch. Every player was in the quarterback position each game.

During halftimes, Sean and his friend Ben could frequently be seen doing the routines with the cheerleaders on the field. They had the moves and sometimes it was a toss-up whether to be a football player or a cheerleader.

Rick was thrilled when he was able to take a Challenger team to Disney World in Florida for the Pop Warner Super Bowl each fall. As Rick returned from the first trip I learned that he had lost Sean when they were there.

Sean was a freshman in high school, 14 years old, and they had just finished eating lunch when Rick saw Sean take off running away from him. The Disney World Sports Complex is huge. There were thousands of people milling around. Rick tried to stop him, but Sean was on a mission, and he quickly lost him in the crowd, so he went to security and had a whole team of people looking for him. They called all the buses that were transporting the teams between the sports complex, the hotel, and the parks. The security people at the entrances of the Disney park were even watching out for him. Sean's team was supposed to be watching a team from our local league as they competed for the National Championship in their division. An hour later a security guard finally found Sean standing outside the Cheerleader Competition Arena. Sean was with a group of cheerleaders striking up a conversation with the girls. Rick didn't tell me this story until they got home, and when he told me where they found Sean, all I said was, "Well, duh! That's the *first* place I would have looked for him."

Video Games

I know what you are thinking. Video games are not a sport and are blamed for the childhood obesity epidemic in our country. If Sean didn't have Down syndrome I would have discouraged video games, but for social reasons, I actually encouraged them. I felt it was important that he knew how to play them so he could play with friends when they came over.

His favorite games were the sports games. Because of first the Game-Cube, then X-Box, and now Wii, he knows the rules for every sport much more in-depth than he learned by playing challenger sports. He also knows the team names and the key players' names too, since they use real teams and real players on the sports games. We did make him earn video-game-time for good behavior and for completing assignments at school and doing chores so he didn't spend all of his time with a controller in his hand. Sean's skills on the video games are impressive, and he is a contender with any other young adult who plays him.

Bleacher Therapy

We all have a personal pool of quicksand inside us where we begin to sink and need friends and family to find us and remind us of all the good that has been and will be. — Regina Brett

Having a sporting event to watch each week was fun. But I had no idea what an amazing support network we were building at the same time. In the beginning we had soccer in the fall, Challenger Baseball in the spring, bowling in the summer. Basketball in winter and summer, then later, flag football would take the place of soccer in the fall. Karate was all year-round. Sean also played Special Olympics Golf and that overlapped with baseball season. We were covered with parental support in the stands all year-round by the time Sean was in high school.

Sean's teaching staff was not on board with inclusive education in high school, and sadly, I had a new story to share almost every week. I will always be thankful for the collaboration of the parents who were also encountering the same attitudes limiting the opportunities for their children in school as well. We had a built-in support group each week, and could brainstorm solutions together. Nobody else could ever understand what we were going through trying to include our children in regular education—we were walking in the same cleats.

Atlantoaxial Instability

It is a mathematical fact that 50 percent of all doctors graduate in the bottom half of their class. — Unknown

Atlantoaxial Instability—AAI— is more common in people with Down syndrome. According to Kathleen Fergus on About.com: The top of the spinal cord is a thick tube-like structure that starts at the base of the brain and runs all the way down the back to the lumbar region. The spinal cord contains the body's nerves or neurons. Vertebrae are the bones shaped in a column in the back of the body that protect the spinal cord. Cervical vertebrae are located in the neck and are abbreviated as C1–C7. The first one is C1 and is referred to as the atlas vertebrae, and the next one is C2 referred to as the axis vertebrae. Misalignment between the two is referred to as atlantoaxial instability, or AAI. Vertebrae are held in place by muscles and ligaments. Since people with Down syndrome have low muscle tone and lax ligaments, their vertebrae can become misaligned causing AAI. 10 percent to 20 percent of people with Down syndrome have AAI, but only 1 percent–2 percent have symptomatic AAI.

Before I signed Sean up for gymnastics at 2½ years old I completed the AAI X-ray screening that was recommended by the National Down Syndrome Society's Health Care Guidelines. The same pediatrician who thought the guidelines were too aggressive, and who told me, "Ten years from now and thousands of dollars later it won't make a difference" about the vitamins called me and said, "X-rays look fine; go ahead and sign him up for gymnastics."

Six years later, we were signing Sean up for Special Olympics and sent the required health form to the pediatrician. (The new and improved pediatrician, that is.) She went back into Sean's records to find the radiologist's report and called me. "I know how diligent you are about Sean's health care. What do you remember being told when the X-ray was done?"

I responded, "I remember the other pediatrician telling me that it was fine and okay to sign him up for gymnastics, or I would have never done that."

She said, "It said, 'Inconclusive, repeat in 1 year.'"

I would have waited to sign Sean up for gymnastics till the X-ray was repeated had I known that. She wrote the referral for a new X-ray, and 2 days after the X-ray was performed, the pediatrician called in a panic. "The radiologist's report shows severe AAI."

She banned Sean from *any* sports until we could see the orthopedist. We were at the end of baseball season and had a trampoline in our backyard. At this point in Sean's 8 years of life, he had been enrolled in 4 years of gymnastics, played soccer, baseball, basketball, volleyball, rode a bike, scooter, and we had annual passes to Disneyland where had ridden many roller coasters. BASICALLY, he had been put at risk for over 6 years due to a pediatrician who editorialized a radiology report.

I called the orthopedic surgeon the pediatrician had recommended and found a 3-week wait for an appointment. With my panicked thoughts of impending paralysis, as well as trying to keep an active kid from harming himself, I asked for an appointment with an associate orthopedist who could see Sean sooner. What a mistake that was.

The doctor entered the room, looked at Sean sitting on the exam table, and asked me, "Why are you here?" I explained Sean had a screening X-ray for AAI and it appeared his had it.

"What's AAI?" asked the doctor.

My first red flag—I mispronounced atlantoaxial instability.

"Do you have patients with Down syndrome?"

He answered, "Yes, but they are older than your son. He must have a mild case; his face looks really good."

I had had it with doctors who were "practicing" by this point in my son's 8-year-old life. So I didn't hold back. "You realize everyone who has Down syndrome has an extra 21st chromosome, right?"

"Yes, but his facial features are so nonsevere. He must have a mild case."

Second red flag.

Next he put the X-rays on the screen and began putting pencil marks on the vertebrae and making measurements. My confidence already was not very high. Then the doctor left the room . . . and returned with a book. Was the book for my benefit? Was the book for his benefit?

Third red flag. He showed me a page in the textbook that I completely didn't understand. But what I did understand as I looked at the X-ray was there was a huge, massive, Grand Canyon-sized gap between the top two vertebrae that was larger than the gap between the other vertebrae. So, pointing at the gap I asked, "Is this space supposed to be so far apart?"

The doctor said, "Don't you think you need some space so you can move your neck back and forth?"

Fourth red flag. "Don't you think . . ." I prefer physicians who *know*.

If you are reading this and you are a doctor, here's a piece of advice—never preface something with "Don't you think." All I could think is, "Don't you *KNOW*?" I asked the doctor if he could have his associate (the doctor we should have seen in the first place) review the X-rays and include his comments on the report. The other orthopedist concurred that Sean did not have AAI. The doctor never physically examined Sean, who I had pulled out of school for this appointment. He never talked to him. He only looked at his "attractive" facial features from across the room.

After the orthopedist's diagnosis that nothing was wrong—in contrast with the radiologist's report that said everything was wrong—I thought we needed a third opinion.

I have an acquaintance whose son had actually had AAI *AND* had surgery fusing his vertebrae. That fall I saw her at a soccer game and got the name of the doctor who had performed her son's surgery, then called the new and improved pediatrician and obtained a referral. This doctor was a neurosurgeon.

I was immediately impressed with the neurosurgeon. He didn't talk to me, he talked to Sean—his patient. He had a conversation with Sean about school, his sports, and his dogs. And then he examined Sean. *THEN* he talked to me. *THEN* he looked at the X-rays. And *THEN* he asked if he could take the radiology report, the orthopedist report, and create a presentation to present on how three different specialties can look at the same thing and have a completely different diagnosis. The orthopedist was wrong. My son had AAI. *Severe* AAI. The neurosurgeon scheduled a CAT scan, where he could be present to position Sean himself, and diagnosed him with a 9mm gap between his first and second vertebra. (According to pubmed.gov, normal ranges are between 3.9mm to 5.6mm in pediatric patients.) *BUT* there were no signs that Sean's spinal cord was compressed. His AAI is in the majority that is asymptomatic.

The neurosurgeon explained that if Sean complained of neck pain, changed his gait, if we tickled him near his belly button and he didn't feel it or his reflexes were hypersensitive, those were all signs that the vertebrae were slipping and compressing his spinal column. We immediately got rid of the trampoline, stopped riding rough roller coasters, and stopped dreaming of Sean's future NFL career. Oh, and no more gymnastics. He also said, "It would be good to avoid a whiplash injury." I have had a couple of whiplash injuries—I would have liked to have been able to avoid them too.

I truly believe that us not knowing Sean had AAI was to his benefit. The amount of physical activity he had enjoyed up to this point had improved his muscle tone so much that I believe that is why he didn't have any slippage of the vertebrae. His muscles and ligaments were holding everything in place.

At this point he has not needed surgery, his vertebrae have not misaligned. We watch for the symptoms and if he complains that his back hurt I immediately lightly tickle his belly button to see if he cand feel it. The gap will always be there, and the possibility that the vertebrae will become misaligned will always exist. But Sean's life didn't stop. He still plays noncontact sports and is very active.

The Grand Canyon Train

Life is either a daring adventure or nothing. To keep our faces toward change and behave like free spirits in the presence of fate is strength undefeatable—Helen Keller

We arrived in Williams, Arizona, on a Thursday evening, and checked into our hotel. We were going to take the Grand Canyon Railway the next day. Sean was 8 years old. After dinner that evening we walked around Williams and came upon a Wild West Gunfight in the street. Sean thought the cowboys were real, and they gave him an empty bullet casing and showed him how to blow into it to make it whistle. The next morning we went to the Wild West Show before boarding the train . . . Entertaining us were the same marauding cowboys we met the night before.

The train ride to the Grand Canyon was very enjoyable. Several roaming musicians performed for us. The fiddler even let Sean play his fiddle—hand over hand. Everybody was very friendly and talked to Sean and allowed him to be a volunteer entertainer every time he raised his hand—which was every time they asked for a volunteer.

The Grand Canyon was spectacular. We spent the night at the rim, and the next day we headed back to Williams on the train. We thought we were close to our destination when all of a sudden the train stopped in the middle of nowhere. Our porter announced the train was being robbed by bandits! He explained that the train stopped for the bandits because it was hard to pay them minimum wage and convince them to jump onto a *moving* train. (Sean didn't catch that part.)

Suddenly, there they were outside our window—bandanas over their faces—riding their horses and shooting their guns in the air next to the train. Sean's eyes were huge. He looked at me and said, "Oh, crap." I had given him some money to spend at the Grand Canyon and he had chosen to save it—he wanted to buy a new video game when we returned home. He quickly handed me his wallet and said, "Hide it!"

I pulled one dollar out of his wallet and told him to give it to the bandits and tell them that that was all the money he had.

We could see them coming into the train car ahead of us through the glass door. The anticipation was almost too much for Sean. Then the bandits rushed through our train car's door.

Sean threw his hands up, waving his dollar, and said, "Here! All I got!" He gave them his one dollar bill. This was the same cowboy we had seen Friday night, Saturday morning, and now for the third time—but with the bandana covering his face Sean didn't recognize him. He squinted at Sean and said, "You sure, boy? This is *all* you got?" Sean just nodded and looked down.

A little while later the "sheriff" (another one of the cowboys) came through our train car. Sean was real excited, jumping up and pointing to the back of the train, "They went there. Got my dollar."

The sheriff said, "Even if I catch 'em, don't expect to ever see that dollar again."

Rick was getting the biggest kick out of Sean believing the bandits were real. When we got back to the hotel room later he had to keep the experience going.

"Sean, did you check your suitcase to make sure the bad guys didn't take anything?"

Sean's eyes got huge. "Oh, crap! My Game Boy!" He grabbed his suitcase and started throwing everything out of it, one article of clothing at a time. When he found his Game Boy (on the bottom), he was relieved and said, "Nope, nothing gone."

Rick pretended to check his bag, and his eyes got big, and he said to Sean, "Oh no. They stole my socks and underwear."

Sean said, "Oh, crap." He picked up a pair of his boxers and socks off the floor and handed them to Rick. "Have mine."

Rick told that story for months afterward. Sean was so sweet and unselfish to give Dad his tiny socks and boxers.

Renaissance Faire

I got a lot of support from my parents. That's the one thing I always appreciated. They didn't tell me I was being stupid; they told me I was being funny.—Jim Carrey

Sean had become good friends with one of his fourth-grade classmates. His mother invited Sean and me to go to the Renaissance Faire with them. I had not been to a Renaissance Faire in many years, and Sean had never been to one. When we arrived, she decided to rent costumes for herself and her children. I decided I didn't want to be a wench, so I didn't rent one, but Sean was really into dressing up. As we looked through the various costumes I saw the jester's costume, and I laughed—in medieval times, jesters were frequently people with Down syndrome. (Many think this is insulting—but with Sean's sense of humor I can see why they were the ones to entertain the royalty and make them laugh.) So Sean donned the jester costume and off we went 500 years into the past, to a time of plagues and pestilences. We were no more than 50 feet into the faire and encountered a band of merry men, drinking mead and greeting the faire-going-folk. They saw Sean's costume and one said, "Fool! Tell us a joke."

Sean pulled out his favorite, "Knock-Knock."

All seven men in unison said, "Who's there?"

"Boo."

Again, in unison, "Boo Who?"

"Don't cry."

They roared with laughter, and Sean decided that this was his kind of world. In the Renaissance, people like Sean were not in institutions, they lived among the people and entertained in the king's castle.

What I Never Thought I Needed to Know about Hypothyroidism

The mistakes made by doctors are innumerable. They err habitually on the side of optimism as to treatment, of pessimism as to the outcome. —Samuel Butler

In fifth grade Sean memorized his times tables through the 5s. The rest of the class was learning fractions while Sean was still working on his times tables. Sean approached his teacher and said, "Teach me factions too." By being exposed to the regular curriculum, he became interested, and he was actually able to learn fractions, and later add fractions too. He loved math and could perform equations easier than he could read text. He was having a banner year academically and behaviorally.

The annual blood screening ordered during his physical just before his twelfth birthday in October returned positive for hypothyroidism. Since this condition is so common in Down syndrome, I was certain I was not going to have to educate any endocrinologist we were referred to, so I didn't read up, search the Internet, or even ask my friends whose children had already received the diagnosis. The endocrinologist advised Sean's pediatrician to put him on Synthroid, and then we were to set an appointment to see him in 4 months.

Sean was having outstanding behavior in school. Everything was coming together. His speech was more intelligible, he had great friendships in class, his teacher was amazing. It was going to be his best year yet . . . until the endocrinologist inappropriately took him off of his thyroid medication.

At the endocrinology appointment in February, 4 months later, this wonderful medical professional drew me a diagram of the thyroid and explained what was going on in the gland's function. I was very impressed with the amount of time he took with us. Then he told me Sean would be off of Synthroid for 4 weeks, and then retested to confirm he had hypothyroidism.

I questioned the endocrinologist. I told him that I had once heard a doctor, who was a specialist with patients with Down syndrome, say that everybody with Down syndrome at some point will have thyroid issues. I explained that Sean had had some significant weight gain before starting the Synthroid, and then lost that weight once he was started on the drug.

His response, "Well, you don't want him on a drug if he doesn't need it."

I agreed with that rationale and discontinued the Synthroid as ordered.

The endocrinologist gave me no warning of possible behavioral signs to look for. And I had not researched it, so when Sean began having *issues* at school, we attributed it to puberty. Full-blown puberty. Big-time puberty.

Puberty from hell.

After the removal of the Synthroid, Sean became a brat; he was angry, he started running away again. The home to school to home communication notebook that had simple entries of "good day today," "great day today," was now coming home with pages and pages detailing Sean's emotional mood swings, behavioral outbursts, telling his teacher, "I'm sad," crying for no apparent reason, and his new inability to complete his assignments.

Four weeks later, as Sean was being suspended from school for hitting a campus supervisor, something he had *NEVER* done, I saw the note in my calendar reminding me to take Sean to have his thyroid test blood draw.

It began to dawn on me that this behavior could possibly be related to being taken off the medication. I had not correlated his behavior to the removal of the Synthroid. I searched the Internet about hypothyroidism, and lo and behold, there it was—"depression, anxiety, mood swings, anger, fatigue, weight gain." (He had also gone up one pant waist-size in 1 month.)

I took Sean to have his blood drawn, then waited a week and phoned the endocrinologist for the results. Sean needed to get back on Synthroid ASAP. After leaving four messages on the endocrinologist's nurse's voice mail, I phoned the pediatrician, and she was wonderful enough to track down the endocrinologist. He informed her of his policy of returning phone calls every other Friday (it was a Monday), and he would call me on Friday. That day Sean was suspended for another day of school for, once again, hitting another adult at school. I left three more messages for the endocrinologist, to no avail.

On Thursday, in desperation, I called the pharmacy to see if there were any refills left on Sean's original prescription, and hallelujah—there were. I then faxed a letter to the endocrinologist's office asking for the results of the blood test and informing them I would be starting Sean back on Synthroid the next day.

One of the endocrinologist's staff called me back and sarcastically told me the doctor had sent me a letter—a letter I have never received. And I never received a phone call on Friday.

After a referral to a different endocrinologist, Sean's dosage of Synthroid needed to be corrected. Sean still had intermittent mood swings, and the new endocrinologist informed me that many people with Down syndrome and hypothyroidism also need a psychiatrist. Thank goodness Sean never did, but "I" could have used one that month.

The moral of this story is: Do not skip your child's annual thyroid screenings (and at 6 months and 1 year for infants) and don't assume their behavior and weight gain is puberty if you have not had the thyroid test performed. Also, never believe *you* can stop learning. Remember, doctors are still "practicing." Behavior at school can be caused by medical issues, so when there are sudden changes in behavior that can't be otherwise explained, look to the medical world for answers.

Years later, our insurance required that instead of Synthroid a generic substitute be used. Sean had some immediate emotional outbursts, and once we switched back to Synthroid, they subsided.

While Sean did get suspended for good cause, the school staff never once suggested he be removed from regular education. A good thing that came out of the behavioral outbursts was Sean's teacher instituted a new positive behavior program for him. She created play money with Sean's photo on it and called it "McMoney." Sean earned it throughout the day for making good choices and completing his work. He was able to choose to "not" complete his work, but if he did, then he had to pay for the idle time with his cash. If he hit someone, then he forfeited all the cash he had accumulated. We followed through with the money at home, requiring him to pay for playing his video games and watching TV. It was a great motivator for Sean.

What I Learned from the (UN) Real Housewives

The easiest way for your children to learn about money is for you not to have any. — Katharine Whitehorn

I walked into the IEP meeting as everyone was roaring with laughter. It was the end of fifth grade, and I knew everyone except one woman attending the meeting. I asked, "What's so funny?"

The principal could hardly speak she was laughing so hard, and she breathlessly said, "She asked if you were the same McElwees as the ones on the television show *The Real Housewives of Orange County*."

The (UN) Real Housewives of Orange County was airing its first season, and I had promised my friends, who were neighbors of these women, that I would not to watch the show. They were embarrassed by the behavior of the stars of the show and believed if nobody watched the show it would be cancelled and their neighborhood would be spared the pending reputation. They had properly warned me—but now I was curious.

For years we had lived parallel lives with *those* McElwees. When Sean was a newborn, his doctor's office nurse brought in a chart and said, "Oh, you're not a 3-year-old girl." Once Rick came home with their dry cleaning—too bad her clothes were too small for me, they were pretty nice. Then the one time I went to the jeweler where Rick purchased my wedding ring to get it repaired. They put "McElwee" into their computer and were happy I was there, and consequently, were very nice to me.

So, I had to *see* them. Those elusive McElwees I had heard so much about. The McElwees who had great taste in clothing and made the jeweler happy to see them—so I tuned in.

Well, the *Housewives* all worked outside the home—right—that's not a housewife—and they threw money around like . . . well . . . When I was raised in Texas, we just called those people, "White Trash with Cash." 'Cause anyone could drill an oil well, but that didn't give them class just because they were overnight millionaires.

But the most eye-opening thing about them to me was their kids— I say "kids." They were 16 to 20 years old—and on camera were so disrespectful to their mothers. *AND* their mothers waited on them hand and foot. Their *kids* had no household responsibilities or chores at all.

After viewing my first episode I called one of my friends to confess I had betrayed our agreement to boycott the show. Her 14-year-old daughter answered the phone and said, "Mom can't come to the phone, she's doing the dishes." And my eyes opened further.

When *I* was 14, *I* was doing the dishes and couldn't come to the phone till *I* was done. I vacuumed, pulled weeds. (When I learned about the existence of Roundup I was mad.) I washed windows—every pane of the true-divided lights in that house. And I decided that Sean would do chores too. We decided to attach money to the chores and combine two goals at the same time: learning money and learning to clean the house.

Allowance

When you've got them by their wallets, their hearts and minds will follow. — Fern Naito

I had been told repeatedly that people with intellectual disabilities had difficulty learning money. So I didn't think we could start too early. When Sean was 5 years old, I started giving him $5 a week. At age 6, he got $6 a week, and a $1 raise each year. I wanted to teach him good financial habits so he could be more responsible with money than *I* had been. We gave him three jars to divide his money into. One jar held the money to spend, one for savings, and one for tithes—he so disliked giving his money to God. We talked about being a cheerful giver . . . He still didn't like giving his money away.

The great thing about having your own money is you can buy anything you want—as long as you have enough of it. When we went into stores, as any child would do, Sean would say, "I want _____." (Usually, every item that was in view at that moment in time.)

I found myself telling him, "You can buy it. Did you bring enough money with you?" It stopped so many arguments about wanting stuff he didn't need—and the biggest revelation to me was that many times—even though he *did* have enough money—he would choose to *not* buy the item he had just asked for. The things he did buy with his own money he really appreciated and took care of far more than things I bought for him.

After watching one episode of *The (UN) Real Housewives* I decided he needed to be more financially independent, and he needed to be learning chores—I was doing him no favors *not* teaching him how to clean the house. There is no way he would ever be able to afford a house-keeper. So, I created a list, gave each chore a dollar value, and began the process of side-by-side teaching him *how* to rinse the dishes, load the dishwasher, run the dishwasher. (Yep, some glasses and plates got broken along the way—and then he learned how to use a dustpan and broom too.) He vacuumed, got the mail, took the trash cans to the street on trash day, he fed his dogs, scooped their poop—and he learned to do his laundry, including changing the sheets on his bed. If we had a problem getting him to do anything at all, it was added to the checklist. When it was time to buy school clothes I would double, triple, or quadruple the amounts he could earn so he would have more money. He didn't *have* to do all the chores, but he only got paid for the ones he chose to do. By the time he was a senior in high school, he *could* earn $100 a week *if* he did all his chores—he never earned the entire $100.

Chore	Earn	Monday	Tuesday	Wednesday	Thursday	Friday	Saturday	Sunday
Brush teeth	.25							
Deodorant	.25							
Dogs water	.25							
Dishes in sink	.25							
Rinse dishes	.50							
Dishes in dishwasher	.50							
Feed dogs	.25							
Get the mail	.25							
Shower	.50							
Brush teeth	.25							
Laundry	5.00							
Trash cans to street	1.00							
Scoop poop	5.00							
Vacuum	5.00							

At age 11, for 6 months I walked him through the steps of doing his laundry every Saturday morning. After 6 months, he knew the steps well, and he was on his own. He made the same mistakes we all made when we started doing our own laundry. He washed his iPod. And to make sure he remembered to clean out his pockets, I had him spend his hard-earned chore money to buy a new iPod. A year or so later he washed his cell phone and had to use his own money to buy a new one too. With natural consequences, he learned to check his pockets. His 48-year-old dad was still learning that lesson. Natural consequences are the best teacher.

By the time he was 12, he could do more on his own than *The (UN) Real Housewives* typical sons and daughters could at age 20. I apparently knew what *I* was doing. So, I made him financially responsible for all of his expenses. He paid for lunch at school out of his own money. He bought his own clothes. He paid for his own movies and outings. I never said *no,* I just asked, "Do you have enough money?"

My friends thought I was awful. They lectured me that it was *my* responsibility to provide those things for him. I reminded them it was still my money, he was just given responsibility to earn it—to learn at an early age that when you run out of money it's gone till the next payday—a lesson I should have learned before getting my first credit card.

Saving and Spending

Money can't buy you happiness, but it does bring you a more pleas-ant form of misery.—Spike Milligan

Sean had a Nintendo Game Cube and wanted an Xbox 360. He begged me for one, but I didn't see why anybody needed two gaming systems, so I told him to save his money and buy it for himself. I took him to the store to see how much it cost. $299.99. He started saving his money. He was 12 years old, and it was June when he started saving.

So he could earn more money I showed him how he could col-lect plastic bottles and aluminum cans and get money for recycling them. He became pretty independent at the recycling center behind our local grocery store. I would drive him there and sit in the car while he emptied the bags of bottles and cans into their trash cans and waited his turn to get them weighed. The girl that worked there was very nice to Sean. I later found out she had a younger brother with Down syndrome. After walking him through the steps of taking the recycling receipt into the store to get the money at the cash reg-ister I started letting him go in and do it by himself. He was so proud of himself for knowing the steps and getting his money all by himself. (This is our regularly shopped grocery store and the employees knew Sean, so I didn't have to worry about somebody cheating him.)

He saved every dollar he made and didn't spend his money on anything for a few months, then he broke down and bought one used

Game Cube game, that set him back about $20.

He got some money for his birthday. By October, he was getting close to his goal.

By the beginning of December he had saved $220 of the $299 he needed to buy the Xbox Game system that included 2 wireless controllers.

A local realtor scheduled and advertised a neighborhood garage sale, so Sean gathered up old toys he had not played with in a while. I took him to the donut shop, and he bought 2 dozen donuts, and he sold donuts and used toys and earned another $50 that day, still just $20 shy of the $299 he needed. I reminded him there would be sales tax too, another $24. So I asked Sean if Dad and I made up the difference would he be OK for that to be a Christmas present from us . . . but we had to wrap it and put it under the tree.

He agreed, so under our tree there was a Xbox 360 wrapped in a gift bag with a tag that said, "To Sean, From Sean, Mom and Dad." Every time somebody came over to our house that Christmas season he walked over to the tree, pulled the tissue paper off the top of the gift bag—and said, "There's my Xbox." His grandparents and cousins loaded him up with games, and he was one happy camper. We were so proud of him for his determination and diligence for saving for 6 months to buy it, and he cherished that Xbox 360 and took great care of it.

After exhibiting such determination to save for the Xbox 360, I was sure we had been successful in instilling responsible spending habits.

I couldn't have been more wrong.

Privacy

Privacy is not something that I'm merely entitled to, it's an absolute prerequisite. —Marlon Brando

It is so much easier to do things *for* Sean than to teach him how to do them for himself. But to do things for him doesn't teach him anything in the long run—and he would fight me too. Our house was a lot less stressful when he learned how to toilet, bathe, and dress himself.

I attended one of Terri Couwenhoven's preconference sessions at the National Down Syndrome Congress Convention in Anaheim, California. She stressed the importance of learning the concept of privacy. I learned from her that as long as we were still helping Sean in the bathroom with toileting and bathing, that it would be hard for him to learn the concept of privacy. In her book *Teaching Children with Down Syndrome about Their Bodies, Boundaries, and Sexuality* (which every parent should have in their library—it also is informative for any intellectual disability, not just Down syndrome), Terri discusses the need to teach a child privacy concepts in four areas of life: body, places at home and in the community, topics of conversation, and behaviors (masturbation). We also took a lesson from Dennis McGuire and Brian Chicoine's *Mental Wellness in Adults with Down Syndrome* and added the appropriate places for *self-talk*.

After attending the conference we began the final steps of teaching Sean how to wash his hair and to wipe his bottom thoroughly.

Then we would close the door and tell him, "You are naked, you need privacy." When he hit puberty and I would catch him touching himself, I would send him to his bedroom, nicely telling him, "That's private time. The only place you can do *that* is in *your* bedroom or bathroom." Stressing *your* because there have been stories of adults with intellectual disabilities who have been having "private time" in *public* restrooms.

Chicoine and McGuire's book was also helpful to understand why Sean would have full-blown conversations in his bathroom before or after his shower. Chapter 8, "Self-talk, Imaginary Friends, and Fantasy Life," told us that if we just sat outside the bathroom door we could learn everything that happened in Sean's day. He would talk out everything that had happened that day, and in the mornings I would hear him talking to his imaginary friends, or was it an imaginary sports team? He would say, "OK, guys, let's do this." Then come bolting out of the door. Everybody needs a little pep talk to start their day, right?

Sean still will sing to his iPod while walking to the bus, or dance and sing at the bus stop. I have shown him other people doing that as we drive past them, and he thinks they look weird. Then I remind him that he does that too, but he can't believe that he looks that strange. We are still working on this awareness.

Sean will tell people lies—or his fantasies. On vacation he was in the Jacuzzi talking to a woman. After she got out of the water she came over and introduced herself to me and asked if I really had 20 children. *Seriously?* Sean can spin some yarns as long as he has someone's ear to bend. I was asked what the consequences were for these tall tales he would spin. Basically—just a scolding from me. Sadly, there was more positive reinforcement by the amazement of the gullible people listening to him and being too nice to call him out. I had to remind him he had a pretty incredible life that he could talk about instead of making things up.

Fantasy is a big part of Sean's world. We just have to learn to manage it. When he was 15 we went to the National Down Syndrome Congress Convention together. He shared a hotel room with a friend, and I shared the connecting room with his friend's mother. The two boys fought the whole weekend over which one of them was Troy Bolton. (Zac Efron's character from *High School Musical*.) They both had basketball tank tops with "Bolton" emblazoned on the back and "Wild Cats" on the front; replicas from the movie. We made them wait until Sunday to wear the shirts to the conference. As they both entered the foyer where the teens and adults with Down syndrome were gathered waiting for the doors to their convention to open, I heard a hundred girls screaming—as though the *REAL* Troy Bolton had just entered the room. The Beatles didn't experience the level of screaming that Sean and his friend did that day. That did nothing for squashing that fantasy. Today, the two boys are friends, and they both have girlfriends so I think they are past being "Troy."

Sean still dreams of moving to Los Angeles to live with his fantasy celebrity girlfriend, Victoria Justice. I didn't help that one much when I purchased backstage passes at one of her concerts so he could meet her. I'll never make that mistake again. When he hasn't met the celebrity-girlfriend-of-the-day, then I can say, "You don't even know her, you don't have her phone number, how can you be dating her?" But after he has actually met her, well, I had to change it to, "She never calls you or goes anywhere with you." As I am writing this he wants to move to New York for some diva there.

Sometimes we had to intervene on the clothing choices. If Sean received a lot of compliments on a new shirt, he wanted to wear that shirt *every day*. If we weren't paying attention, then he would get away with it. Then sometimes in the summer he wanted to wear a hooded sweatshirt or in the dead of winter (in Southern California it can be in the 40s early in the morning), he would want to wear a tank top to show off his muscles. If we told him to change clothes he would stall and argue with us. We had to instead tell him we weren't leaving until he changed, then give him a choice of two shirts that were acceptable. We had to just sit down and wait him out until he would finally acquiesce. "Fine. I'll do it." If we argued and tried to reason with him, everything just took longer. I called it "reasoning with the unreasonable" or "feeding the monster." The more we argued and tried to reason with him, the more he argued back, got agitated and angry, and the longer it would take to get him to change his shirt. If we simply shut up and ignored his pleas for wearing the inappropriate garment, the monster wasn't fed on the words, and he wasn't angry.

Now I simply remove the tank tops from his closet during the winter and remove the sweatshirts in the summer. When he becomes obsessed with a clothing item and wants to wear it every day I sneak into his room and remove it, or make him wash it every day if he has different places to go that won't notice he is wearing the same thing day after day.

Discovery

To an adolescent, there is nothing in the world more embarrassing than a parent.—Dave Barry

Just wait till the "hair down there" appears—that was a fun night—Sean was 12 and had been independent in the bathroom for a while so I was unaware that the "hair down there" had arrived. Sean was preparing to take a shower when he started screaming, "MOM! QUICK! MOM! COME HERE!" I ran upstairs to his bathroom completely expecting to see blood, and as I unlocked the bathroom door from the outside (love that little tool that allows you to unlock locked doors), there he was standing with a washcloth in his hand. He said, "It won't come off." He was trying to wash off "the hair."

I had given him the video titled *Where Did I Come From?* which is a cartoon narrated by Howie Mandel about changes in your body at puberty, making babies, etc. It was at the level of understanding that Sean was at—just enough information, but no "instructions" on how the act of making babies is performed. When they *penciled in* the cartoon hair, apparently Sean didn't relate that to actual hair.

Trying *SO HARD NOT TO LAUGH*, I said, "Oh, you're becoming a man. Just like the movie, you're growing hair. There will be more hair in your armpits one day, and maybe on your chest." Then thinking to myself, *But not if you take after Dad.*

From then on he watched his armpits, and lo and behold, the summer he was almost 16 years old there it was—and he proudly said, "Mom, look." As he took his shirt off and lifted his arms. "Armpit hair."

Ah, a proud moment.

Buddy Sitters

Meeting the world with a loving heart will determine what we find there. — Gregory Boyle

The school district provided no after-school day care during intermediate school. I still worked full time but needed some sort of supervision for Sean after school each day. I wanted him to have as *normal* of an after-school life as possible. I was lucky he had three good friends who agreed to be Sean's Buddy Sitters.

One of the boys' mothers committed to picking up Sean each day along with his designated buddy sitter and bringing them to our house. They would arrive at our house around 3:30, and we were always home by 5:00. They were to get a snack (we left several choices each day to choose from), and then just play—basketball on the driveway, video games, whatever—but fun was the point.

The schedule was set, and the boys made $5 an hour. We paid them when we got home. If there was a minimum day and they were there longer, then they were paid for the additional hours too.

These three boys were extremely responsible. One time one of them was sick and he called the other two boys and arranged for one of them to fill in for him the next day—then he called me and explained who would be with Sean and why. This was a great responsibility for the boys, an opportunity to make money, and they all had fun with Sean. It also helped Sean to feel like he was home alone without us there and it was the beginning of us feeling like we might be able to start leaving him home alone.

Communication Is Key

My cell phone is my best friend. It's my lifeline to the outside world.
—Carrie Underwood

Sean was in seventh grade, and I discovered Verizon Wireless had a cell phone called the Mi-Go. This phone had four buttons you preprogrammed with the important phone numbers, and had a GPS tracking feature. It was pretty limited, but at that age it was perfect for our needs. It came with a companion phone that I could use to search Sean's whereabouts, and it would tell me the address where the phone was located as long as it was turned on. Sean was instructed to *NEVER* turn it off. Like with the walkie-talkies, he was supposed to call us to let us know which neighbor's house he was visiting. He was also instructed that he must always answer the phone.

This phone gave me the guts to let him go, and gave Sean the confidence that he could be rescued with one push of a button. We started by letting him go to the neighbor's house and call me to tell me where he was. Then to the park across the street—to join a pickup game of basketball. Then to walk to Taco Bell four blocks away.

Having the Mi-Go also gave us the courage to start leaving him home alone. We started by leaving for a very short time. We would call the entire neighborhood to let them know that we were running to the store for 20 minutes and have them watch out for Sean. We next went out to dinner alone. It was great to go on dates and not have to pay a babysitter.

We slowly extended the amount of time we were gone over a 3-year period of time. We got to the point that if it was a nonschool day we could get up and go to work while Sean was still asleep. He could get up, make his breakfast, take his pills (we would leave those sorted out for him in a cup), and entertain himself for several hours. The beginning to all of this independence was made possible by the advent of the cell phone with GPS.

UCLA Pathway—College for Students with Disabilities

When I left home to attend the program two years ago, I had no idea of how life-changing my experience would be.—Courtney Vinson, Pathway Graduate

Today, when a parent of a younger child with Down syndrome asks me what is the number one thing I wish I had known when Sean was born, my answer is, "I wish I had known to save for college." Sean was entering seventh grade, and I heard about a program that was starting at UCLA for adults with disabilities. I gathered some other moms who were also curious, and we set an appointment with the executive director, Eric Latham. Although our children were around 12 years old and a few years away from potentially applying, Eric spent 2 hours answering our questions and giving us a tour.

We learned that the program isn't just about academics, it's about giving the "college experience" to students with disabilities. This was their first semester of the program. They had one student whose reading level was at the first-grade level, but in their literature class they were employing adaptive technology, and this student was listening to the books they were reading on a CD. The students have the opportunity to take extension classes, and one student was taking photography. The sports programs had adopted their group, and the students were riding the buses to the Rose Bowl for the football games, along with the typical UCLA students.

Instead of living in dorms, the Pathway students were living in two-bedroom apartments across the street from the dorms. Their life skills were being provided through Regional Center Funded Supported Living Services, and an independent agency sent the support staff to work with the students after school hours.

Eric said they had needed to do some training with those people and gave a great example of a group of girls who wanted to get manicures. The support person had gotten the phone book out, found a local nail salon, called, and set the appointment for the girls, and off they went to get their manicures. Two weeks later, the girls needed their nails done again, so the support person repeated the steps. Eric said they had to teach the support person that she needed to be "teaching" the girls the steps to set their own appointment and not "doing" it for them.

The second year of the program, the students had to work in a job that they were interested in. Sean had already decided he wanted to be an usher at Angel Stadium, and I asked Eric if being an usher at UCLA sporting events was a possibility, and he said it was. Wonderful, the program was individualized.

This was the kind of training and independence I wanted for Sean. It fit our goals perfectly, but the cost didn't fit our budget. I wanted to prepare Sean in case we hit the lotto, or could find some funding source in the future.

As five mothers grilled Eric about safety, curriculum, and daily living supports, I asked what they were looking for in their students.

They wanted a well-rounded student. Eric said they were very disappointed in the quality of the transition programs and high school programs that they were seeing. He said while they want to see the students' IEPs, they were not placing much weight on them because they were so poorly written. Grades also didn't count. What they were looking for was a student who was independent, a student who *wanted* to be there, and a family who wanted their student to be independent.

He told a story of interviewing students separate from their families and finding some had no intention of moving out of their parents' house. Then there were the parents who were hesitant and were not ready to let their student go just yet. He told us that overnight experiences away from home were very heavily weighted in the application process. Volunteer experiences also were heavily weighted because many of our kids don't get paying jobs that young, but also work experiences with their transition programs were looked at with favor.

The program was also instilling a huge sense of giving back in their students. People with intellectual disabilities are part of a population that is heavily served, but totally capable of giving back. He told us of a beach cleanup that they had planned, and the students were completely organizing it along with a local nonprofit agency. The event had not happened yet, but he was excited about what the public's perceptions would be when they received their instructions, trash bag, and gloves from the Pathway students. His enthusiasm was infectious and I saw a positive future for Sean.

Today, there is a great Web site, www.thinkcollege.net, that lists all of the college programs available for students with disabilities nationally. As of this writing, there are 232 choices. Amazing progress had been made, all because of inclusive education.

After touring this program we looked for opportunities for Sean to volunteer, camps he could attend, and other opportunities to foster his independence to prepare him for a college program in the future.

Volunteering

Anybody can be great because anybody can serve. You don't have to make your subject and verb agree to serve. You don't need a college degree to serve. You only need a heart filled with grace and a soul generated by love. — Dr. Martin Luther King Jr.

After visiting the UCLA Pathway Program I looked at everything Sean did with different eyes. We were seeking volunteer opportunities. He had already had one volunteer job that had been an interesting experience.

When Sean was 10, he told us he wanted to be a greeter at our church. The Greeting Ministry enthusiastically included him, gave him a volunteer name badge, and positioned him at the top of the outdoor staircase they nicknamed, "Heart Attack Hill." Most people as they crested the top of the stairs were so out of breath they could barely talk. Sean shared the station with a woman, Patty, and she would say, "Welcome to Saddleback," and Sean would shake their hand. They made a great team since Sean's articulation still wasn't intelligible to everybody. This arrangement worked great for a few weeks . . . until Sean decided the breathless Christians needed a pat on the back. But he was so short that he couldn't reach their backs, so he was giving them pats on their bottoms. As Rick and I sat nearby supervising we saw both women and men get a startled look on their face, then turn and realize it was Sean who had just patted them on their bottom. Most of the time they would then grin, but sometimes not. We tried to explain to Sean that they didn't need a pat, but he continued to insist on a little gluteal slap. Sean's stent as a greeter quickly ended. Sometimes not every endeavor works out, and having the tenacity to move on to the next thing without dwelling on an unsuccessful venture or being embarrassed is important.

The Down Syndrome Association of Orange County provided great volunteer opportunities for Sean. He is a pretty good golfer, so starting the spring after we visited UCLA, Sean performed the Ceremonial First Drive at their annual fundraising golf tournament. (Holding fundraising events for people with disabilities without including them as part of the event is counterproductive and creates a pitying atmosphere.) Later, Sean helped with the fundraiser's Live Auction, delivering the prizes to the winners of the bids. One year, I caught him placing bids on the silent auction items. I realized what he was doing, as he was trying out a putter he had put a bid in on. I had to look at all of the bid sheets—over 100 items, to cross his name off. He also tried to participate in the live auction that night too, holding his paddle up for every item up for bid.

The Down Syndrome Association of Orange County's annual Buddy Walk gave Sean the opportunity to fund raise, and he had his own team. He was able to raise $1,200 one year and $1,500 the next year, then $2,000 the following year, beating his goal each year. Then the DSAOC started an All-Star Team, and the teens and adults with Down syndrome would lead the Buddy Walk. Sean was signed up and took charge, carrying the banner, and earning himself a photographic place on the promotional materials for future Buddy Walks.

Sean became Santa's Helper, wearing an elf hat for the annual Breakfast with Santa that the DSAOC held. He helped Santa with the children, passed out candy canes to the kids and their families, and distracted the babies to get them to look at him in his elf hat, instead of Santa for photos. The first few years it was the same Santa, and he asked whether his helper would be there each year. It was a great experience for Sean and for the parents of the little ones to see that their kids one day could grow up and give back too. By the time he was 16, we were pretty sure he didn't still *believe* in Santa anymore. When we asked, "What do you want Santa to bring you for Christmas?" his response was, "I'm too old for Santa now."

We arrived to the event early for his volunteer duty. Santa arrived early too. Sean introduced himself and shook Santa's hand and explained that he would be helping him out that morning. Then he said, "Santa, can I ask you something?"

Santa said, "Of course."

Sean asked, "Santa, am I too old for you?"

"Ho! Ho! Ho! No, Sean, you'll never been too old for me."

Sean jumped in the air, pumped his fist, and shouted, "YES. I want an iPhone and a new NFL Football Wii game for Christmas."

When he was 20 we were leaving the event and Santa was thanking Sean for his help. Sean pointed both his fingers at Santa—pistol-style—and said, "You're welcome, Santa, and don't forget—Guitar." Santa glanced my way and said, "Did you get that, Mom?" Whew, I almost missed that one.

When Sean was 15 he began serving in the children's ministry at our church in the 10-year-old and younger class for children with disabilities. While our church is inclusive, there are special classes for the students who have sensory issues or need a smaller setting on

Sunday mornings. Sean still volunteers and has been in this role for over 6 years, inspiring parents and gaining more patience with the children.

We tried volunteering for the Meals Ministry and served dinner as a family to volunteers at the multiple Christmas services at church. Sean spent more time visiting with the volunteers and Rick and I did most of the serving, so we didn't sign up for that one again.

In high school I was the Exceptional Child Committee Chairperson for the PTSA and had Sean help by stamping students' cards at registration. Sean's classmates saw him as a contributing member of the school in this role.

All of these volunteer opportunities gave Sean a sense of what it would be like to have a job, and in each experience he was able to gain confidence in trying new things.

Sean Outsells Adults

Efficiency is for robots — be effective. — Mike Rowe

A large, local, nonprofit agency holds an awareness festival made up of nonprofit agencies who serve children over the Labor Day Weekend every year at one of our malls. It allows families who are doing their back-to-school shopping the ability to learn about what services the various agencies provide that could help their children. Between the back-to-school shoppers and people looking for a place to cool off on a 90-degree day, the mall was packed.

Adult volunteers from the Down Syndrome Association had manned their booth on Saturday, and the goal was to sign up people for our local Buddy Walk along with identifying families who have members with Down syndrome, who may not know about our DSA. Anybody who signed up for our Buddy Walk received an Anaheim Angels Baseball cap as a gratuity.

All day on Saturday the adults didn't sign one person up for the Buddy Walk. On Sunday, Sean and I arrived at 12 noon, set up the booth, and Sean took six hats and stood in the aisle and asked every person who walked by, "Want a Free Hat?" If they said yes, he pointed to me and said, "Talk to Mom."

In 40 minutes we had 19 people signed up for the Buddy Walk. I called the program director and told her we only had six hats left and another hour and a half to go. She quickly brought over 25 more hats and sat there and laughed as Sean reeled in more and more people.

When we left at 2 p.m., there were only seven hats left. We had signed up 43 people for the Buddy Walk who knew nothing about Down syndrome and just thought it would be fun to spend a day *IN* the Anaheim Angels' Stadium and walk where only Angels tread. All of these people would become aware of Down syndrome by being present at the Buddy Walk, and Sean spread positive awareness with his selling skills that day in the mall.

Camp Increases Independence

Camp is the only place where "you're so weird" is considered a compliment—#Campconfessions

When Sean was in seventh grade he started going to Young Life's Capernaum Club every week. (Our club was called High Rollers.) I attended Young Life in high school, and it was a fantastic, wholesome, nondenominational Christian experience. It was always a lot of fun and full of loving young adults who truly care about teens. Sean loved the singing time and the skits, and he was making a lot of friends who also had disabilities.

When he was in ninth grade, I let him go to their 1-week-long, overnight, summer camp. (Note: Sean didn't attend eighth grade, so ninth grade was right after seventh grade for him; he was 14 years old.) Attending camp was going to fulfill the requirement of overnight experiences away from home for qualifying for the UCLA Pathway Program if we decided later that he should apply to the program.

He needed some pajamas for the camp, so we were on our way to Target to buy some. He said, "I want seven pajamas." I asked him how much money he had brought with him. He took out his wallet and counted $17.

"That's not enough money for seven pairs of pajamas."

He said, "No, you buy." I laughed and told him I had paid for the camp, he had to pay for the pajamas. Because it was his own money, he carefully looked at the sales rack and ended up with two pairs of pajamas on sale for $12 total. I still thought we had successfully in-stilled responsible spending habits.

The camp was inclusive and had typical teenagers and teens with intellectual disabilities there. He had a one-on-one camp counselor who was assigned to do everything with Sean each and every day. The photos showed Sean doing things he had never done before, and he had a blast away from his pesky parents.

He came home with a suitcase full of clean clothes. I was morti-fied to find out he had worn the *SAME* clothes—including under-wear—all week. But that had been my mistake. I sent him in a shirt that said, "I Have Down Syndrome—What's Your Excuse?" I had pur-chased this shirt when he was experiencing some educators who had bad behavior in seventh grade. The school had sent a note home that the shirt was offensive and not to send him to school in it again. But it was really pretty funny, so I sent him to camp with it, and they loved it so much and made sure everybody saw it that Sean decided to wear it every day for the entertainment value. The underwear and shorts were just a part of the ensemble.

Every time he went to camp after that I told his counselor to make sure he put on clean clothes every day, and I sent him with sever-al shirts that had different sayings on them. One said, "The More The Merrier," and had the looped chromosome design all over it. Another said, "Looking Good in My Designer Genes." And "Yes, you can Admire my Extra Chromosome, Marvel at my Accomplishments, and be Awed by my Good Looks . . . And YES, You CAN Have my Autograph!"

But something else happened during that camp experience other than wearing the same clothes every day. Sean was empowered, he was more self-confident and braver than ever before.

Summer

Not everything that can be counted counts, and not everything that counts can be counted.—Albert Einstein

When Sean was 14, after he returned from High Rollers' Camp, he worked as a volunteer at a local day camp as a Camper in Leadership Training. He had attended the summer camp as a camper for a couple of years, but now he was too old to attend as a camper. He was still unable to stay home all day all summer by himself, plus that would have been boring. The staff knew him and were thrilled to have him on board.

I had enlisted a service "Inclusion Connection" that was funded by our Regional Center (Department of Developmental Disabilities) and was administrated by our local United Cerebral Palsy Association to provide a one-on-one aide who acted as a "job coach" for him during the Camper in Leadership Training job. Ironically, the aide they placed with Sean had worked at that camp the prior summer as a camp counselor. With that extra support Sean and the camp had a very positive experience. Being in charge of the children continued empowering Sean and building his confidence, and mine, that he could handle more responsibility and independence.

Operation House Call

He is the best physician who is the most ingenious inspirer of hope.
—Samuel Taylor Coleridge

When Sean was 8 years old we signed up for a program called Operation House Call through the Area Board IX Office of the California State Council on Developmental Disabilities. Each spring, two first-year medical students from the University of California Irvine Medical School would come to visit the home of a person who has a developmental disability to learn firsthand about that disability, what it was like to be a person with the disability, what their family life was like and the medical problems that person may have experienced. They also learned from the parents of their experiences with the medical professionals they had encountered.

While this gave me an opportunity to educate these future physicians by telling the stories about the myriad of medical professionals we had encountered—the good, the bad, and the ugly—Sean loved having two young adults that were completely paying attention to him.

He always started by taking them to his room to show them the over 50 sports trophies he had collected from his many sports leagues. Also, he showed them his Special Olympics medals, and his growing sports memorabilia collection of autographed pictures, baseballs, and hats.

Then he would challenge them to play a video game with him— and Sean would beat them handily every time. (They wouldn't be good medical students if they played video games all the time.) He flirted shamelessly with the female students.

I would usually field their questions, but when Sean was 14 years old, I finally decided that he was old enough that he should be answering their questions, so I gave them permission to ask Sean anything they wanted to. The first question *EVERY TIME* (especially when they would find out he was in regular education classes) would be, "Are the other kids mean to you?" Sean was always surprised by that question because the answer is "No." He couldn't imagine why his friends would be mean to him.

When he was in seventh grade the two medical students that came to our house were both originally from the San Francisco Bay Area. We reminded Sean that he's been there a few times and asked if he remembered the big bridge we walked across. He asked, "Golden Gate?" It had been over 3 years since we were last there, so I was glad he remembered.

When he was a sophomore the students asked him, "What's it like to have Down syndrome?" Sean thought for a moment, then answered, "Down syndrome . . . it's a disability . . . but it's no big deal."

As those students were about to leave they said something that really showed me this program was worth it. "We studied genetics, and we'll probably forget a lot of what we learned, but we'll never forget Sean, and he will be our reference for our patients with Down syndrome." These future medical professionals will make great doctors—mission accomplished.

New York City

New York is the meeting place of the peoples, the only city where you can hardly find a typical American. —Djuna Barnes

I have no idea what Sean saw on TV or heard at school that made him want to go to New York City so badly, but he persisted for 2 years, continually asking to go, so by his fourteenth birthday in his freshman year of high school, the stars aligned, and I was able to make it work.

I had a two-for-one airline ticket and hotel points so I made the offer, "Would you rather have a birthday party *or* go with me to New York City?" Sean didn't hesitate in enthusiastically replying, "NEW YORK CITY."

And so the planning began. I looked on the National Down Syndrome Society (NDSS) Web site and found out their annual Buddy Walk was the weekend before Sean's birthday. I sent in a photo from our vacation the previous spring of Sean on a zipline in Costa Rica for their annual Public Service Announcement on the giant Panasonic TV in Times Square.

Of course, a Broadway show was on the agenda so we hit the Web and checked out hits including *Grease, Mary Poppins,* and *Wicked*—Sean chose *Wicked*—hands down.

We chose a bus tour and booked a cruise to see the Statue of Liberty.

The big day finally came. Rick and I gave Sean a digital camera for his birthday, and he immediately started snapping pictures.

The NDSS had e-mailed that the spokespeople for the Buddy Walk, Chris Burke and John C. McGinley, were scheduled to be on the *Today Show* Friday a.m. We made plans to stand outside the studio for that show.

Sean took pictures of the entire trip, including the people arranging our transportation to the hotel. He photographed the people checking us in at the Marriott Marquis Hotel that evening, and then we went to explore the Times Square neighborhood.

We found the Today Show Studio, and there were a few hundred people already lined up. We asked why they were lined up the night before the show and found out that Bruce Springsteen was going to perform in the street the next day, and they expected 10,000 people to be there. I was pretty sure that we weren't going to be able to get anywhere near the studio the next morning. Sean was determined that we try—even though he had no clue who "The Boss" was. As we walked the four blocks back to the hotel Sean just stopped halfway through a block, said his feet hurt, and he couldn't make it the next 2½ blocks. Ugh, the big stop, drop and flop. I had to coax him to the corner. We got lucky and found a pedicab that could take us the rest of the way, and it was fun too.

The next morning I made the decision not to wake Sean up too early. While Bruce Springsteen is cool, grumpy Sean is not, and I knew that Chris and John weren't scheduled to be on until the end of the *Today Show.* He woke up around 7:30, and we took off, picked up some McDonald's (or as Sean called it, "Old McDonald's") and went to take a chance on seeing Bruce. We got lucky—well, Sean got us lucky. I had made a large sign that said:

BUDDYWALK'd
All the way from
CALIFORNIA

We were holding hands, and Sean was carrying the sign and we approached the security guard near the stage. I asked, "Can we come in here?" He took one look at Sean holding the sign and said "Yes, come right in." Score—another Disability Discount moment.

Bruce Springsteen's concert was awesome. Holding our sign, Sean and I got on TV several times as they segued before and after the commercials. When Bruce started his last song, Sean said, "Let's dance." So we started to swing dance and got on TV again. I called and e-mailed my mother and friends who were all in later time zones and would be able to see us on the show. I had my work BlackBerry with me and got an e-mail from a coworker in Pennsylvania that said, "Did I just see you dancing on the *Today Show*?" I later saw the clip and have no idea how she knew it was me, the whole thing was less than 5 seconds long.

We saw Chris Burke and John McGinley on the TV monitors, and Sean was excited that his heroes were on the other side of the window we stood outside of.

Soon, we headed out to the tour bus to see the sights. Empire State Building, The Broadway Bull, Diamond District, the street that Carrie on *Sex in the City* lives on; we drove past so much that was new to us yet very familiar at the same time. We decided to skip Ground Zero. We were within a block of it, but we were having so much fun I couldn't bear to go.

Lunch was eaten at a hot dog cart in Battery Park. Sean loved that. His favorite food at the time was hot dogs, and to get one on every corner he thought was the best thing ever.

We took a cruise to see the Brooklyn Bridge and the Statue of Liberty. Sean was surprised at how big the Statue of Liberty is. He made friends with several people on the boat, including two men from Holland. (Hmm, could that be a coincidence?)

After that, we went back to the hotel and took a nap, then headed out for some authentic New York pizza. As we left the hotel we were approached and offered tickets to an Improv Comedy show at the Laugh Factory. They assured us it would be G rated.

We had our slice of pizza, it was great, then off to the Laugh Factory. Of course, when the audience participation request was made, Sean's hand went right up, and that landed him on stage. He was assigned to make sound effects while the comedians improvised to Sean's sound effects. They then asked the audience for an occupation and Sean yelled, "Do Mom's job."

They asked what I did and I replied, "I sell medical devices."

So, they pretended to have a box of medical devices, picking each one up, and Sean made sounds like, *"Boom. Bang. Spush."* And they played off of those sounds. Their creativity was very funny. The audience went wild.

But then they brought out a "new" comedian who was trying material out on us. He was "OK" . . . until he got to his story about a Southern motel's continental breakfast. His joke included a mother with her *mongoloid* children. The whole room groaned out loud, then went silent. I got my coat and purse and tried to get Sean to leave. He said, "No, Mom, this guy's funny." That's when I realized that he had never heard the word and didn't even *know* he was being insulted. The audience didn't even clap for this guy, and he ducked behind the curtain before I could introduce him to Sean and give him a piece of my mind. I didn't tell Sean what that word meant. I don't think it is something that would make anything about his life better.

On Saturday we slept late, ate a late breakfast, did a little shopping around Times Square, then headed down to Broadway to see *Wicked*. What a well-written, amazingly performed, fantastic moral of a story.

Sunday morning came, and Sean was very excited that his cousins were coming from Connecticut to spend the day with us. But first we walked across the street from our hotel to Junior's Restaurant for breakfast. We sat inside and on the other side of the window sitting outside was a family with a very cute blond girl with Down syndrome. Sean immediately started flirting with her through the window and told me, "I'm going to marry her." After we finished eating we went outside to meet them. They too were there for the NDSS's Public Service Announcement Video and had driven in from outside the city.

When my sister and two of my nieces arrived we walked two

blocks to the Giant Panasonic TV and joined the rest of the families of children with Down syndrome to view the National Down Syndrome Society's Public Service Announcement featuring all of our children's beautiful faces doing everyday things. As each family's child's photo came up cheers were heard. Sean was so excited to see his picture so big on that TV in Times Square.

We headed to the Great Hill in Central Park. When John McGinley spoke he said 4,000 people were there in the park for the Buddy Walk. That was their biggest Buddy Walk to date.

Chris Burke spoke, some cheerleaders did a cheer, and then the walk began. All along the walk cheerleaders were positioned at each turn and cheered us on. Each time we passed the cheerleaders Sean would make the telephone sign with his hand up to his ear and say, "Call me." He was flirting all day.

Entertainment from the stage included a guitarist with Down syndrome, Signing Times performed singing and signing songs. The area was packed with parents and their younger children. Then Laz D, the rapper with Down syndrome, got up to perform. The parents with the younger children scattered, and the teens and young adults were ready to dance. After Laz D was Chris Burke, John and Joe Demasi's band, and they performed a couple of songs. There were a lot of talented people with Down syndrome showcased that day.

We went with my sister to her home in Connecticut so Sean could see his uncle and other cousin who had been at her ballet rehearsal for an upcoming performance of *The Nutcracker*.

Sean had a lot of fun while playing with his cousins. His uncle drove us back into the city that night. Monday we headed home. On the plane I asked Sean if he had a good birthday weekend, and he answered, "YES." I asked him, "What was the best thing you did all weekend?" His answer, "Playing with my cousins." At least he has his priorities in the right place.

First Fishing Trip

Don't follow your passion. Always bring it with you. Don't leave home without it. — Mike Rowe *(Dirty Jobs)*

Rick goes fishing every fall with the guys to a lake in the Sierra Nevada Mountains . . . they CAMP—tents, no running water, no toilets, what I call *dirt camping*. Sean was 15, and Rick decided it was time to take him with *the men*.

After they arrived and set up camp, Sean kept sneaking into Rick's car and calling me from his cell phone. Funny thing, Rick told me that cell phones didn't get a signal there.

Sean was filling me in on the trip. He would report, "The tents are up." The next call would be "Mom, we have to poop outside." I was laughing so hard. Rick had no idea he was calling me with all of the reports.

The second day of the trip the weather turned bad on them, and unfortunately, there was a full-blown *BLIZZARD*. Being *Real Men*, they wanted to wait it out so they could fish. But it got worse, and finally when the snow was blowing sideways they decided to pack it up and come home.

While they were taking down the tents Sean called me again and said, "Mom. *WE'RE DOOMED. WE'RE STUCK IN THE MIDDLE OF NOWHERE, ITS SNOWING AND WE'RE DOOMED.*" I died laughing, he was so dramatic. I said, "Sean, you have a truck, you can drive out of there." He said, "Oh. All right." Rick has invited him on trips since then, but for some reason he always says, "No, thanks, Dad."

Sean's Way Out

Drive carefully. It's not only cars that can be recalled by their maker.
— Robert Fulghum

Sean and Rick went on a father-son weekend—which gave me some great time to get caught up at home.

They were heading out to Lake Havasu to stay at a friend's house. After they arrived Rick called me proudly, "Sean got me out of a ticket." I was angry that he was speeding in the first place. "Oh, wasn't he scared when you were pulled over?" "No, the officer came up to the passenger-side window because we were on the highway. I gave him my driver's license and while I was digging in the glove box for the insurance and registration, Sean stuck his hand out of the window to shake his hand and said, 'Hi, I'm Sean, and this is my dad, Rick.' The officer started grinning, handed me my license back, and said, 'Keep it to the speed limit.' I could see his shoulders shaking he was laughing so hard as he walked back to his car."

Hugging

The best and most beautiful things cannot be seen or touched—they must be felt with the heart.—Helen Keller

I'm not sure why people think you are supposed to hug people with Down syndrome, but it's an epidemic. I'm more of a hand-shaker than a hugger, so I don't feel comfortable hugging complete strangers, or even acquaintances.

I laughed the hardest at the movie *The Ringer* when Stevie is identified as "Not a Hugger," then goes on to fake having an intellectual disability to compete in the Special Olympics—where hugging is a key part of the sport.

From the beginning we have had several professionals tell us to curb the hugging behavior because it would make Sean vulnerable to sexual predators and lower his boundaries for hugging strangers.

It didn't work. Sean *is* a hugger. He loves to hug and be hugged. It was a constant battle to teach Sean who it was OK to hug, and how to discriminate who was a friend and who was a stranger. Sean knew no strangers. We had our friends and family shake his hand to eliminate the confusion. And then some complete stranger would decide to hug *him*, and we would have to begin the "no hugging" learning process all over again.

Our church has greeters who shake hands and high-five people as they arrive on campus. One Sunday morning this new greeting couple had taken the station where we entered the church campus.

And they both enthusiastically hugged Sean and welcomed him. They didn't hug everyone, only Sean. And he loved it.

We directed Sean to shake hands, and they said, "Oh, it's OK, we love to hug." One incident like that and Sean was back to hugging *everyone*.

The next weekend they were there again. I had to ask them to *not* hug Sean again and explained that it made him vulnerable. They acquiesced but the damage was done; the lesson had to be re-taught.

Sean was in his sophomore year of high school as we entered the stadium for the football game. The students *all* greeted each other with hugs. And Sean was hugged as well. I've never seen a group of kids that were so into hugging, but I finally gave up. I didn't want to teach 3,000 teens not to hug Sean. It was a beautiful thing to see how accepting and loving they all were toward him and each other.

Tim Harris, a young adult with Down syndrome, has done nothing to quash the hugging stereotype. Owning his own restaurant where hugs are on the menu, *Tim's Place* has become a destination. YouTube videos of him hugging President Obama went viral, and news of an upcoming reality TV series is a testament that hugging isn't criminal. I, for one, can't wait to see Tim's hugs on television.

Winter Formal

Each friend represents a world in us, a world possibly not born until they arrive, and it is only by this meeting that a new world is born.
—Anais Nin

During Sean's sophomore year two girls knocked on our door with balloons and a big poster that said, "Will You Go to Winter Formal with Us?" One of our neighbors, Ashley, and her friend, invited Sean to go with their group of friends—14 teens—in a Hummer limousine to Winter Formal. Of course, Sean said "YES." He jumped up and down, then he hugged the two girls individually, then both at the same time.

WELL, Ashley found out the *NEXT* day that her GPA for first semester was only 1.83—she was usually a B student, but blew it the first semester that year. The school's policy was you can't go to the dances if your GPA is below 2.0.

I found out after the fact that she went into the assistant principal's office, crying—not upset that *SHE* couldn't go, but upset about how this would affect Sean since she's the one in the group that he knew the best. She explained to the assistant principal (while crying), "I don't care that I can't go to Winter Formal, but I invited Sean McElwee, and he's going to be so disappointed." I'm not sure which assistant principal it was, but he replied, "Sean's my buddy. You guys are going to have a blast." Then he waved his magic wand and removed the restriction so she could buy the dance ticket. Her mother was blown away and told her daughter, "It's just because of Sean that you are getting to go to Winter Formal." Neither her mom nor the school would have let her go because of those grades. I think you could say that Sean was a "Friend with Benefits," and Ashley benefited from the "Disability Discount."

The Winter Formal was a lot of fun, Sean went to dinner with the group beforehand, and then rode in the Hummer limo to the dance, then had dessert at an after-party with the group. Then his junior year he went to Winter Formal with this same group of kids in a limo—again. As a mom, I felt so *normal* not knowing what happened that night—other than the report that Sean danced in the limo the entire way to dinner and the dance and back afterward.

Summer between Sophomore and Junior Year

A man on foot, on horseback or on a bicycle will see more, feel more, enjoy more in one mile than the motorized tourists can in a hundred miles. — Edward Abbey

Summer was all set, Sean was to experience his second year as a camper in leadership training. The camp decided that he didn't really need a "job coach" again and I listened to them, and not my conscience—and on the third day of Sean's summer volunteer job he was "excused." I was told he could return if he had an aide. Of course, it was too late to request and get funding for an aide approved after summer had already started.

I asked Sean what happened and he said, "He didn't listen to me."

Turns out they left Sean *alone* with a group of 6-year-olds—I thought he was in "leadership training" not "leadership." One of the kids didn't listen to Sean, and so Sean got angry . . . and pushed the child down. Thank goodness the child wasn't hurt, but he was scared— rightfully so. For the next couple of weeks when Sean chose not to listen to me, I asked him if I should push him down, and he totally understood why his choice was the wrong one. I was impressed they would even consider letting him return under any circumstances. But no aide was to be had, so the piecing of the summer schedule began.

One of my good friends, Kristi, agreed to pick Sean up at noon each day to take him to the local community center for an afternoon of fun with her son and their other friends. The first day, Sean got himself ready, even packed his lunch, and waited for her to pick him up. He had a lot of fun at the community center and was looking forward to going there again the next day. When he woke up the second day he was so excited to get to the community center that he couldn't wait till noon to get to the fun—but I didn't know of his plans.

Around 11 a.m., I called our home phone number to remind him that Kristi would be there in 1 hour to pick him up to be sure he would be ready. There was no answer, so I called his cell phone.

A side note about cell phones—they not only were a lifesaver, they also gave Sean so much more independence than his friends had. Think of them more as an assistive technology device than a luxury for a child. Sean's first cell phone had a GPS tracking system that linked to my phone, and I could find him even if he couldn't tell me where he was—we never had to activate the search function, but it gave great peace of mind to know we could if we had to.

Sean answered his cell phone so I reminded him that his ride would be there in 1 hour to pick him up and his breathless response was, "I'm almost there, Mom."

And so the discussion went, "Almost where?"

"The Community Center."

"What? Are you walking?"

"YEP."

"What street are you near?"

"I'm almost there."

"Sean, they don't open for another hour. Kristi's going to pick you up at our house. Can you walk back home?"

"Nope, I'm almost *THERE!*"

Click. He hung up on me. I called back, he didn't answer. He pushed the button to send me to voice mail.

Thankfully I was between appointments for work, and only 15 minutes from home, so I quickly drove to our neighborhood, and started at the community center driving the route backward toward our house—hoping and praying that he was going the right way on the *2-MILE* walk.

As I turned the corner to enter the busiest street in the journey, there he was with his lunch box trudging along in the 85-degree heat. Instead of picking him up I decided to spy and see if he knew how to get to the community center, and if he was safely crossing the streets. He turned the correct corner and was going in the right direction. He met up with another teen walking down the sidewalk. He thought nothing of Sean being there, walking down the street, alone. As they walked down the block they seemed to be having quite an in-depth conversation, and at the corner the teen went a different way. Sean pushed the crosswalk button and waited for the "walk" sign to flash, then looked both ways and properly crossed the street. (Sean later told me that the teen was one of the players on the varsity baseball team that he was the assistant for in high school.) He totally knew where he was going and had the whole situation under control. I picked him up in the parking lot of the community center and took him back home till noon. It was only 11:30, and he had 30 more minutes till they opened. Determination to get to the fun was his motivation. And my confidence that he could safely enjoy more freedom was growing.

The High School Musical Haircut

Who would ever want to be normal? Normal can never be amazing.
—Mini Cooper advertisement

Was I ever sick and tired of the songs on the soundtracks of both *High School Musical 1 and 2!*

Sean was obsessed, but I guess there are worse things to be obsessed with. (It took him 4 years to get over Barney the Dinosaur after I finally hid the tapes at age 8.) He was so obsessed with *High School Musical* he even wanted his hair cut like Zac Efron, the lead actor who plays the character of Troy Bolton.

Sean was independent at the hair salon by now. I would sit down and look at magazines while he would go up to the counter, check in, and instruct the stylist on what he wanted his hair to look like, pay, and most of the time give a tip without a reminder from me. Sean took the picture from the cover of his *High School Musical 2* CD to the hairstylist to show her how he wanted her to cut his hair. But first he had to tease her, so he pointed to the photo of Corbin Bleu (who is an African American and has some great long Jheri curls on his head).

The hairstylist didn't skip a beat. She said, "You're going to have to buy a wig for that hairstyle."

Sean laughed, then pointed to Zack's hair and the cutting began. Every day after that he looked into the mirror to make sure it was smoothed down in front and styled exactly the same as Zac Efron's hair in the movies.

Self-Determination

Here's to freedom, cheers to art. Here's to having an excellent adventure and may the stopping never start. —Jason Mraz

Self-Determination—self-de-ter-min-na-tion (self-di-tur-muh-ney-shuhn, self-) noun
1. Determination by oneself or itself, without outside influence.
2. Freedom to live as one chooses, or to act or decide without consulting another or others.

Self-determination is synonymous with independence. Sean was getting a taste of freedom and taking more opportunities to exert his self-determination and not exactly asking for permission. A few weeks after his 2-mile walk to the community center we went to Sacramento, California, to Sean's first National Down Syndrome Congress Convention.

Sean and a friend shared a room, and his friend's mother and I shared the adjoining room. I decided to sign up for a preconference session, and so did my roommate—big mistake. We didn't preplan what we would do with the boys while we were learning.

My friend Kristi, the same one who had been driving Sean to the community center all summer, was also attending the conference, but was not signed up for a preconference session. She came through for me again and said she would pick up the boys at our hotel and walk them the two blocks to her hotel and go swimming and we could pick them up when we were done with our sessions.

Sean and his roommate were instructed to stay in their room. Room service was going to deliver their breakfast at 9 a.m., then at 10 a.m., Kristi was going to come to get them and walk them the two blocks to her hotel—and this is where the fun began.

There was a break in my preconference session around 9:30, so I called Sean to remind him she would be there in 30 minutes. Sean didn't answer, so I checked with Kristi, and she said that her son and Sean had talked on the phone and Sean knew she would be there soon. Then Sean called me back. I asked, "Are you in your swim trunks yet?"

He said, "Yep, and I'm swimming too."

"Where are you swimming?"

"In our hotel."

"How did you find the pool?"

Sean, sounding annoyed that I was so dumb, "The elevator said where it was."

This was a high-rise hotel a block from the Capitol, and the pool was indoors on the fourth floor.

"Well, stay there. I'll tell Kristi to pick you up there."

I called Kristi as she was leaving her hotel and said she would go get them from the pool at my hotel. I went back into my preconference session, and my phone began to vibrate. Sean was the caller, so I left the room and answered. He was upset, "Mom, the key won't work."

"The key to what?"

"Our room."

"Aren't you still at the pool?"

"No, we went back to the room to meet Kristi."

"Oh, take the key to the desk where we checked in. Do you remember that place?"

"Yes."

"Tell them it stopped working and tell them your room number, and they will give you a new one. What's the room number?"

"5636"

"That's right, can you do that?"

"Yes."

"Go there and they will help you."

"OK."

I called Kristi and told her they would be in the room, not the pool after all. *THANK GOD FOR CELL PHONES.*

Here's the story Kristi told me later. She got to their room and Sean's roommate was there, but not Sean. She called Sean's cell. "Where are you?"

"At the hotel."

"Yes, but *where* at the hotel are you? I'm at your room."

"I'm waiting for you."

"Yes, but *where* are you waiting for me?"

"At the hotel."

"Are you inside or outside?"

"Outside."

"OK, stay there, I'll be right down."

Poor Kristi. She had entered the hotel through the back door, and Sean was waiting for her outside the front door. He was wearing his swim trunks . . . that was all . . . no shirt, no shoes. She had to convince him he needed shoes to walk the two blocks on concrete sidewalks to her hotel.

As they came back inside the hotel and passed the front desk the woman behind the desk saw Sean and addressed Kristi and said, "Excuse me, did you hear what happened?"

Kristi said, "No, what?"

"Well, this young man, and his friend came down to the desk. They had locked themselves out of their room, and they had no identification on them, so we had to send Security up to unlock their room, they showed them their identification, and their room keys so Security left them there. I just wanted to make sure everything was all right."

Kristi died laughing and said, "Yes, it is now."

Sean is pretty smart. He knew I would be angry at him for not remembering to take the room key to the pool and therefore locking himself out of his room. So he lied and told me the key didn't work. I guess with as much as we've traveled and had keys that have demagnetized, he thought he'd use that excuse.

Later that night Sean was at the dance. I went to the parent reception, and when I came back, discovered that his date had left, so I asked him if he wanted to leave. I noticed he didn't have his camera. I asked him where his camera was.

"I left it under that table."

It wasn't *under* the table he pointed at—so we looked *under* several tables, and he got upset with himself for losing his camera and before I knew it he was gone. I wasn't sure where he went so I called his cell phone—and a woman answered. She said his phone was on *top* of a table, along with his wallet *and* camera. It was on *TOP* of the same table he said he had left it *UNDER*. She raised her hand so I could find her, then I was scared—Sean was on the streets of Sacramento—no phone, no wallet. But he did have his room key tucked inside his conference badge holder. I went back to the hotel, and THANK GOD, he was in his room and he was in bed. Now, *that's* independence.

The next night when I came to get him from the dance I found him on the dance floor sitting down—with his camera and phone in his hand. I asked him, "What are you doing?"

He answered, very nonchalantly, "Taking pictures of butts."

Oh the honesty. I would have preferred to be lied to that time. I deleted all the pictures of the butts.

Ladies' Man

Follow your own particular dreams. We are handed a life by peers, parents and society. You can do that or follow your own dreams. Life is short, be a dreamer. — Hugh Hefner

Ahh, Sean and girls. He started young with his flirting. Sean was 3 years old, and we were living in Eastern Washington State. One evening we attended a local festival where a band was playing and people were dancing in the street. There was a cluster of four or five teenage girls, who were around 16 years old. Sean went over and was dancing and flirting with them. They thought he was *sooo* cute. And then he did it.

He walked over to one of the girls who was wearing a dress, and lifted up the hem, and took a peek to see what was under there. They all laughed, everybody loved his curiosity . . . and I just said, "That's cute now, but it won't be when he's 16."

Sean was in regular education kindergarten when he came home one day, put a dish towel down on the kitchen floor, and started unloading the refrigerator onto it. Gallon of milk, package of lunch meat, package of cheese, head of lettuce . . . When I asked him what he was doing, his answer, "Picnic with Bictoria."

"Bictoria" was actually "Victoria," but he couldn't pronounce the "V" yet. She had the longest, thickest black hair in the class, and frequently was sent home for lice. But he loved her anyway. At least until first grade. She was very nice to him, and her mother thought the crush was cute. Over the summer Victoria's family moved to another school district so she wasn't there the next year—and thus forgotten.

In first grade he was in love with a little blond girl, and frequently wanted to call her on the phone . . . Thank goodness we didn't have her phone number.

In third AND fourth grade there was Becky, another brunette. In fourth grade Sean cooked up a scheme to be in the school's talent show, doing a magic act. Well, his articulation was pretty bad, so he decided he needed a beautiful assistant . . . Becky.

Here's how the conversation went as we were driving to Disneyland for the day:

"Mom."

"What?"

"Talent show" (pronounced "tawant sew").

"Talent show?"

"Yes."

"What about the talent show?"

"Me do it."

"What do you want to do in the talent show? Sing? Dance?"

"No, MAGIC" (pronounced correctly—with apraxia, the words sometimes come out right).

"Magic?"

"YES."

"OK, we will go to the Disney Magic shop and see what they have before we leave."

A few hours later we were heading toward the exit of the Magic Kingdom, so we stopped by the magic store, and this great lady was working behind the counter. She truly had magical powers as she read my mind. I put my arm around Sean, gesturing with my eyes, and said, "Sean wants to do a magic act for his school's talent show. . . . Do you have anything that *HE* can do?"

She was great. She said, "Well, if you are going to be on stage, you need something that everyone can see. I have two tricks that would be good. Here is a regular rope. Place it on the ground, and say, 'Sit,' then say, 'Stay,' then say, 'Roll over,' and pick it up and turn it over—it's kind of funny—THEN, hold it out in front of you and say, 'lie down,' and it will stay straight out." (It had some sort of wire that allowed it to go straight out when held the right way.) "Then, roll it between your fingers and say, 'Play dead,' and it will flop down, just like a regular rope."

Then she also had the one scarf that you pull and out comes four different colored scarves. The rope trick was great, but if nobody could understand the words, "sit down, roll over, lie down, and play dead," then it didn't make any sense . . . and it wouldn't be funny.

Well, Sean had a plan. I told him we were going to have to practice the words so everybody could understand him.

He said, "Becky help." So, the beautiful assistant was added to the show. And here's how it went: Becky came out on stage first and announced, "Ladies and Gentlemen, I would like to introduce The Magical Sean McElwee the Magician." Sean bowed, and she continued, "Since the Magical Sean speaks Seanese, I will be translating for him."

Sean wore a black robe and a Merlin the Magician Hat complete with long gray hair attached to it. As Sean narrated the tricks, Becky repeated his words into the microphone, as if to translate so everybody could understand him.

After each trick Sean took his bows even before any applause occurred.

After telling the rope to "play dead," the crowd roared with laughter and applause. Sean's act was a huge success. The parents were cracking up even after the show. His was one of the quickest acts, and that made it a big favorite for the parents who sat through over 2 hours of *talent* from the elementary school students.

The best part for Sean? Becky had to come to our house for 2 weeks, two or three times a week, to rehearse, and Sean was in heaven. After their performance, he still wanted her to come over and rehearse.

He still liked Becky in fifth grade, but he kind of liked all the girls in fifth grade.

Halfway through sixth grade a new girl moved to the school, Kimmie. She was added to his inclusive classroom and the teacher sat her in the desk next to Sean. He was assigned the duty of introducing Kimmie to the other students and giving her a tour around the school. Kimmie held his affections through that year and all through seventh grade. In seventh grade she had lunch with him every day. He looked forward to seeing her at lunch, and if a teacher or aide was trying to keep him in class to finish an assignment, or trying to make him change from his PE clothes into his street clothes, they were subject to physical altercations. No one was keeping him from lunch with Kimmie. She was very sweet, blond, and according to Sean, "HOT." All the way through his junior year in high school he would still tell people that Kimmie was his girlfriend. A very sweet girl, she made a huge impact on him.

Trying to stave off the inevitable I told him that he couldn't date till he was18, and he couldn't get married till he's 30 . . . and no sex till he's married . . . so starting at age 13 he would tell people, "My birthday is tomorrow. I'm going to be 30." His next question to any cute girl, "Will you marry me?" Translation: "Will you have sex with me?" Occasionally we would decode his message to the person in question, but most of the time we kept the true meaning to ourselves. Of course, Sean thought sex was kissing . . . because in the G-rated films that's all you would see. He thought that for many years.

I also told him he had to date a girl with Down syndrome or another disability. I remember going to a book signing with Jason Kingsley Mitchell Levitz when their book *Count Us In* came out. Sean was a baby, but it struck me that Mitchell was adamant that he didn't want to date a girl with Down syndrome or any disability. It made me sad that he would likely be alone, and as he grew up I knew Sean would want a long-term relationship.

Two Goals

The biggest adventure you can ever take is to live the life of your dreams. —Oprah Winfrey

Sean was 15, or as he would tell you, "Almost 16." He was planning to attend his first National Down Syndrome Congress Convention. Sean had two goals for the weekend:

1. To find a girlfriend
2. Get kissed

I relaxed the age 18 rule . . . He was on to me by now. At his high school he saw a lot of classmates dating, and even kissing on campus, and they were under 18, so he made it clear to me that rule had to go.

We flew into Sacramento the night before the convention began. The local Down syndrome association had planned an activity for the early arriving convention goers to attend a movie at the IMAX Theatre. We entered the theatre, and Sean promptly began working on his goals for the weekend. He began moving through the seats, shaking hands and introducing himself to EVERY girl in the theatre (before the movie began) and asking how old they were . . . most were over 20, so he kept going till he could find somebody more his age . . . but alas, no success. He said a little too loudly, "Mom, they're all too old." That got a laugh from the parents.

But not all was lost. There was one girl his age that was coming from New Jersey. Her mother and I were friends from an Internet support group we were members of. Her mother and I had connected the two of them, and they had been e-mailing each other all year. He was excited to meet her in person the next day—finally.

The next day, Sean met the Internet friend, and they had dinner and went to the dance the first night together. Unfortunately, she had some sound sensory issues and it was way too loud for her. So she had to leave early. And like many typical blind dates, there was no chemistry or love connection there.

Sean's First Date

On the first date men worry about what they're going to say while women worry about what they're going to wear. — Mario Tomasello

On Saturday, during the conference, I went to pick Sean up from his concurrent conference for lunch, and I arrived just in time. He was leaving the room, holding hands with the *CUTEST* girl, and he pointed to her and said to me, "I'm having lunch with *HER*." About that time her mother arrived on the scene and we asked if we could join them. They allowed us to tag along.

We went into a deli, and Sean told her, as he pulled out his wallet, "You can have *ANYTHING* you want." He ordered the same thing she did, and he hardly ate—way too smitten—and the girl from New Jersey and her family joined us for lunch . . . She was so bummed out that Sean had found another attraction, so I told her, "Sean's a player," and she smiled knowingly.

I asked the newest interest how old she was—and she said, "I'm 18." Oops, since Sean was frequently lying about his age, I asked her if she knew he was 15. She said, "I don't care, he's cute." OK, their priorities were on the same page.

They had a great time dancing that night, but his second goal was not achieved. He didn't get a kiss. She lived about 8 hours away from us so they would talk on the phone, but by the next summer she wasn't interested in him anymore.

After attending the National Down Syndrome Congress Convention with Sean I vowed we would never miss another one. This is an amazing opportunity for teens and adults with Down syndrome to attend their own convention and learn a lot from other people with Down syndrome who teach the sessions they attend. He came out of each convention more mature, more self-confident, and more empowered.

Now, THAT's Social Networking

In Social Media, the "squeaky wheel" gets the oil. You have to put yourself out there, to find people who will relate or even debate with you, depending on what you are looking for.—Jessica Northey

Sean still wanted a full-time girlfriend. While the girl he met at the NDSC Convention was great, she lived 8 hours away in Northern California. He wanted a real girlfriend that he could call, text, go on dates with, get to know better—and kiss.

The TV Show *Glee* was in its first season, and Sean was a huge fan from the first episode. When the "Wheels" episode of *Glee* was aired in November 2009, Sean saw Lauren Potter debut as Becky Jackson and said, "Wow, she's cute. I want to meet her." The following weekend was the Down Syndrome Association of Los Angeles' Buddy Walk and one of his friends was going to lead the walk with his famous brother. Sean's friend had invited him to lead with him. I told Sean that Lauren would probably be there and to look for her at the Buddy Walk.

Unfortunately, I was going to be at a sales meeting and was unable to be there. But I learned all of the juicy details secondhand, from her mom and Rick.

According to my sources, Sean located Lauren quickly. Although there were several hundred people there, he found her sitting on the front row at the performance stage. He sat in a chair directly behind her and began staring a hole into the back of her head. Her mother commented to her husband, "Looks like she's got a fan."

Rick was texting me everything that was happening. "He found the Glee Girl."

Then he sent me a photo of Sean and Lauren on stage with the "chairman" from the television show *Iron Chef*—Mark Dacascos. Mark was a contestant on *Dancing with the Stars* that season and was teaching them some dance moves. After meeting on stage, Sean and Lauren hung out together and were separated when the walk began.

Sean didn't get her phone number, and they went their separate ways that day. I really let Rick have it for not reminding Sean to get her phone number. But he had a good excuse. "I forgot. I haven't had to ask for a phone number in almost 20 years."

Fast-forward 6 weeks and Sean received his invitation to the Down Syndrome Association of Orange County's Annual Red Carpet Ball—their formal dance for teens and adults with Down syndrome. This would be Sean's second ball, and he wanted a date. Not just any date, he wanted Lauren Potter to be his date. He didn't have her phone number, but he remembered that the only connection he had was her Facebook Fan Page. So he wanted to post an invitation on there. He was so nervous, and asked me to type it so here's what he dictated:

Lauren,

I am typing this for my son Sean—he is the guy you danced with on stage at the DSA LA Buddy Walk.

Sean: "Hi, Lauren, Will you go to the DSA Orange County Red Carpet Ball with me? I can pick you up, you can meet me there, whatever. It's on Saturday, February 27, at a hotel somewhere."

Lauren, you can e-mail me? (I inserted my e-mail address.) if you want to find out more or want to go.

Sean loves to dance—oh yea, you already danced with him!

Sandra

And we waited . . . and waited . . . 5 days went by and it was apparent that she was not checking her Fan Page on a regular basis.

NOW, THAT'S SOCIAL NETWORKING ➤

Sean posted again:

Hi, Lauren, Please go to the DSA Orange County Red Carpet Ball with Me? You can e-mail me at (e-mail address).

And I also posted to her:

"Hi, Lauren, in case you don't remember Sean, here is a picture of you and him at the DSALA Buddy Walk."

Now we were full-blown stalkers.

I finally e-mailed Gail Williamson of Down Syndrome in Arts and Media (DSIAM) and asked her to e-mail Lauren's mom and ask her to tell Lauren to check her fan page. And finally there was a response from Lauren, on Sean's Facebook:

"Sounds fun, Sean. I would love to go."

And on my Facebook she posted:

"I love this picture. I do remember Sean. The ball sounds fun."

And the date was inked. But that wasn't enough for Sean. He didn't want to wait another 5 weeks to see Lauren, so he called and invited her to lunch and a movie. She lived 1 hour from our house. I drove him to pick her up. Before he got out of the car he cued the CD to just the right song on the *High School Musical 3* soundtrack. When they got in the car, it started playing from the beginning. She said, "I love this song."

Sean said, "Me too."

We went to lunch. She chose the restaurant Chipotle. I wasn't sure how well she could read, and I knew Sean was very nervous, so I started reading off the board and said, "They have chicken and beef burritos. What do you think you will want?"

139 ➤

Lauren said, "Bean burritos are my favorite."

Sean was astonished and said, "Me too." They were discovering they had so much in common.

I let them have some privacy and sat at a different table reading a book. When everybody was finished eating I told them I was going to the bathroom, and then we would go to the movie. Lauren asked to go with me. When we got into the bathroom she said, "I don't want to hurt his feelings, but I don't think we're going to work out."

I was crushed for Sean, but I also understood—not every romance works out.

"It's OK, Lauren. Not everybody likes each other romantically. But do you still want to go to the Red Carpet Ball as friends?"

"Yes, I do still want to go to the ball, but just as friends."

Later that evening I called her mother to ask what Sean had done to turn her off . . . Well, turns out when they sat down to lunch he said, "Lauren, I love you. I want to marry you."

And she replied, "I'm too young to get married."

We had to have a discussion about being *cool* and *chill* because girls don't like to have it laid on so thick. I also explained that girls don't like the "creepy, clingy guy."

I would tease him when we were out a few times after that to drive the point home. I would put my arm around him and say, "Ohh, Sean, you're so hot, you're so cute, I love you, I want to marry you."

He would pull away from me all creeped out and say, "Stop it." He got the point.

On the night of the Red Carpet Ball Sean knew he was just the "ticket into the ball." I had many friends who were volunteering that night that filled me in on the details.

Lauren sat next to Sean at dinner, but talked mainly to one of the volunteers at the table. When the dancing started she went to dance by herself. Sean would approach her to dance, and she would put her hand up to stop his approach. Sean's a pretty attractive guy, he's fit and athletic. As the night wore on many girls began to notice him, and at one point he was dancing with four girls at one time. Lauren apparently noticed this, and like every girl, decided if all those girls like him, maybe she should reconsider.

We had gone to dinner with her parents and when we returned there was a whole new tone. Sean and Lauren were dancing together and she told her mother, "I like this Hot Dawg."

Courtship with an Extra Chromosome

If you're not living on the edge, you're taking up too much space.
—Anonymous

I had to drive an hour away to pick Lauren up for dates. After a while her mother was nice enough to meet us halfway and that made a big difference. Between her taping schedule, Sean's activities, and the distance between our houses they only saw each other on the weekends. A couple of months into the dating Sean had a basketball clinic that he was going to attend and invited Lauren to come with him. The boys who were holding the clinic were high school age, and almost immediately one of them recognized Lauren and said to his mom, "Mom, she's a Cherrio on *Glee*." Lauren loved being recognized. But she also liked the cute high school boys and immediately began flirting with one named David. I wasn't sure how he would react, but he definitely knew what was going on.

After the clinic we were going to drive Lauren home and visit there for a while. But first, Sean had to take a quick shower. As we pulled into our driveway, he announced to me, "I'm *NOT* going." He took his basketball and headed to the park across the street from our house. I understood that his feelings were hurt.

I told Lauren, "OK, let's get you home."

We drove in silence for a little while, then she said, "I don't like the way Sean disrespected you."

I responded, "He wasn't disrespecting me, his feelings are hurt, so he didn't want to come to your house."

She was oblivious. "Why are his feelings hurt?" I explained that he saw her flirting with David and that made him sad, and then she started talking about another boy from her transition program. A boy who didn't like her (like a girlfriend), but she had a huge crush on him. This was an issue we've had with Sean many times where he "likes" a girl who he has no chance with but believes in his heart that there is a real chance for true romance.

After the 2-hour round-trip I pulled back into our driveway. Sean was playing basketball on our driveway with a neighborhood friend. Rick was walking out of the front door with Sean's cell phone. "Sean, Lauren's on the phone."

I heard Sean's side of the conversation, "Hi, Lauren. No. *NO, Lauren*. You break my heart. No. I won't." Then he handed the phone to *ME*.

I took the phone and Lauren said, "I told him I still want to be friends. He doesn't want to be my friend."

This was so hard for me. On one hand I wanted to be Sean's mom and say, "Why would he? You flirted in front of him." But on the other hand, I knew she didn't realize what she had done. So I explained, "Lauren, I can't make Sean be your friend any more than I can make you be his girlfriend. Give him some time, his feelings are hurt." Wow, was I proud of Sean. Most guys would have taken the doormat position of "friend," and then hang around "hoping" for more. But not Sean, turns out he's an all or nothing guy.

But Sean's stance paid off. A few months later Lauren called him out of the blue and said, "I miss you." And the romance was back on.

Every date held some sort of drama. If they were with a group, Sean didn't like it when she talked to anyone else. If it was just the two of them, Lauren would start to think of another guy and get moody. There seemed to be a point in every date that she would ignore Sean and not talk to him at all, and he would get angry and feel rejected. Once she got an emotional reaction out of him, then she would get all lovey-dovey and reel him back in. And he would go willingly.

They would hug, and sometimes kiss, and he would say, "Oh, Lauren, I love you."

And she responded, "I love you too."

Every date was on an emotional roller coaster, and every date seemed like it would be the last one. I had to stop going on their dates. It was too stressful. So I hired my neighbor's daughter to drive them on dates. Her boyfriend would go too, and it was great—a double date—just what they should have been doing all along.

Sean and Lauren were off and on more times than I can count over a 3-year period. Courtship with an extra chromosome means there are a lot of misunderstandings. When two people have different receptive and expressive language levels it creates constant misunderstandings, which leads to a roller coaster of emotions.

Another thing that happened confused me at first. Sean would remember one of the past breakups and have an emotional response as though it was happening right at that moment. It made no sense to me until I was in one of Dennis McGuire's sessions at a NDSC Convention and he talked about the recall of people with Down syndrome and how they can relive an experience as though it is happening this very moment from a memory. Never believe that people with Down syndrome forget anything.

Prom Party Favors

Only those who will risk going too far can possibly find out how far one can go. —*T. S. Eliot*

Sean had invited his friend Andie to the Best Buddies Prom. She is a great dancer, a lot of fun, and his girlfriend had recently broken his heart and given him the ole, "I just want to be friends."

There were a group of five teens with disabilities and four moms, and we decided to rent a limo . . . Some of the other teens in our group needed more supervision so we all rode in the limo together, and when we arrived at the dance and had successfully dropped the kids off, we were chauffeured to dinner. When the prom was over, we went back, picked Sean and his friends up, and headed back for some dessert at another mom's house. There was a lot of loud music and dancing in the limo on the way home.

On the way back in the limo Andie kept kissing Sean on the cheek . . . He was loving it, but not kissing her back . . . probably because I was sitting right there watching them.

After we had cake I sent a quick text to Andie's mom and told her we would have her home in about 25 minutes. She jokingly texted me back, "Put Andie in the front seat." (Note: Texting and driving was not illegal when this story occurred.)

I drove a van, and they were sitting in the middle bucket seats with a huge space in between them. I texted back, "They are in the in the middle seats—they're bucket seats, so there's a big space between them."

She replied, "I remember what I did in bucket seats."

I sent an, "LOL," and a few minutes later Andie yelled, "*SEAN!* Sandra, *Sean* touched my boobies."

I quickly texted her mom, "Oh-oh, drama in the backseat," while simultaneously yelling, "Andie, you hit him. *Sean.* You apologize. Andie, always hit boys that touch your private body parts."

Andie was confused and said, "I'm not supposed to hit anybody."

Her mom texted, "What's going on?"

I replied, "Don't want to tell you." Then I yelled at Sean again, "*Sean.* You need to apologize. *Andie,* it's OK to hit boys when they try to touch you in your private body parts."

Andie said, "Sean, my dad has a knife."

Texting to her mom I said, "Sean copped a feel, and Andie is holding her own . . . Nobody's taking advantage of her."

I once again yelled at Sean, "Sean, you have to apologize—*now.*" Then I thought, *Well maybe it was an accident . . . They were hugging across the space between the seats . . . Maybe when he pulled away he accidentally "brushed by."* So I asked, "Sean, was that an accident?"

Sean said, "Nope. On purpose, Mom."

I so wanted to laugh. But I had to hold the line on respecting girls.

I texted her mom and told her, "Tell her dad to be in the front yard with the shotgun." And "Andie told Sean he has a knife."

When we pulled into the driveway her parents were in the front yard cracking up laughing. Andie got out of the car and was so mad at Sean. She stormed inside the house.

Her father said, "Sean, I need to talk to you."

Sean jumped out of the car and went right over to him—no fear.

Her dad put his arm around him and pulled him close and said, "Sean, you have to wait till you're married to do that."

Sean said, "Right. Thanks." Sean apologized to Andie, and they are friends again, but she always looks at him sideways when we see her.

###

Sean has a solid goal of getting married. He has frequently proposed to his girlfriends in many different places, usually lacking a ring to go with the proposal. (One girl provided a ring during a proposal.)

In order to get an idea of what it would be like to support Sean one day should he enter into matrimony I attended a parent discussion session at the National Down Syndrome Congress Convention where two couples whose son and daughter had married answered questions and discussed their experiences. My big takeaway was that the marriage was not just between their son and daughter—it included both sets of parents. They explained that with their typical children they had *met* the daughter or son-in-law's parents and saw them at parties and gatherings but didn't have their phone numbers or talk on a regular basis. In contrast, they talked on a daily basis with the parents of their adult child with Down syndrome's spouse. That's when I realized I was going to be married to my future daughter-in-law's parents. After that realization I approached the dating scene with much more caution, not wanting to be yoked to unpleasant or impossible in-laws. Thankfully, so far, we haven't encountered any of those.

Just as Sean has brought angels into our lives, he brought lovely girls and their lovely parents in as well. Philosophies differ though. It amazes me the parents who have fought for inclusion in school but exclude their daughters from living independently and from serious relationships. It has been a true learning experience of respecting the girl's family's beliefs and wishes while supporting Sean's goals.

Relationships are messy with any couple, so why should the relationships of our teens and adults with Down syndrome be any different? Books like *Men Are from Mars, Women Are from Venus* try to make sense of our differences. I know many couples who have been married for years who still struggle to communicate. Marriage therapists are busy for a reason.

In the movie *A League of Their Own*, Tom Hanks implores, "There's no crying in baseball." Well, there *is* crying in dating relationships.

Boys cry, girls cry, and it's normal. *More Alike than Different* isn't just a campaign by the National Down Syndrome Congress when it comes to relationships. Dating is full of drama and emotions; rational and irrational, just as many typical relationships are. Misunderstandings run rampant as communication is difficult with receptive and expressive language differences. It's almost a full-time job to referee what an actual meaning is vs. what was heard. There is never a dull moment, that is for sure.

Sean has a social skills coach who was instrumental in helping him with one girlfriend. They saw her occasionally, and she helped them with their communication issues. It was like couples counseling, but the goal wasn't to stay together but to learn to communicate, and that lesson works in every type of relationship in life, not just in romantic relationships.

Real Independence Includes Transportation

Learning from experience, learning from people, learning from successes and failures, learning from leaders and followers: personality is formed in these reactions to stimuli in social environments. —James MacGregor Burns

I try to use natural supports as much as possible. Natural supports are peers, not educators. Sean was a sophomore and needed to learn how to get home from school on his own. Our school district didn't send a big yellow bus to our neighborhood. (We had opted out of the little yellow special education bus.) The regular education students were required to ride the public bus, so Sean needed to ride the public bus just like everyone else. The students in the special day class were learning to ride the public bus during their classes each day as a part of their life skills education. Since Sean wasn't in that class I needed to arrange for him to learn this skill outside of school.

My neighbor's daughter, Megan, agreed to teach Sean to take the public bus home from school. We started his training 2 months before school ended his sophomore year. Megan would meet him on campus at a place she selected to teach him where to cross the street, and how to wait in line for the public bus.

I paid her $5 per day (she thought $25 a week was awesome—so did I), and I paid for her bus pass. She walked him through the steps for a month. For the next 2 weeks, I told her to have him talk her through the steps. Then I told her to just follow behind him and make sure he was able to do it alone, with no reminders or prompting. Two months from the start, he was independent on the bus, knew where to get off, and *I thought* he knew how to walk the four blocks home. Then she confessed that they actually would go to Taco Bell as soon as they got off the bus, where her mother would pick them up and drive them home. *She* didn't want to walk the four blocks home. So, I had to give her a raise and pay her $10 per day to entice the walking. Her mother still met them and picked up her heavy backpack so she didn't have to walk with it, and she showed Sean the way to walk home. *THEN* he was independent.

But the bad habit of stopping at Taco Bell had started. When school began his junior year, he took the bus home each day and went straight to Taco Bell. He would save enough from his lunch money to get a soda and a bean burrito. He would eventually get home, but many days I would have to stop by Taco Bell on my way home from work and pick him up. I finally caught on to his after-school snacking when he wasn't hungry enough for a healthy dinner. I began to limit the amount of money that he could take—he didn't need that "fourth meal" (Taco Bell's current ad campaign) or the soda every day.

One day Rick was home sick and Sean was supposed to be on the bus home. Sean called, panicking and yelling into his cell phone, "Dad, they didn't wait. The bus left me. They didn't wait."

Rick said, "Wait for what?"

"I was at McDonald's, and they didn't wait for me." Ah another lesson in life: the public bus is not your private taxi service.

Another day he called Rick again. "Dad, I don't know where I am."

"Why?"

"The bus didn't stop. I got off next, but I don't know where I am."

Rick said, "Look around, is there a store?"

"Yes, but I don't know what it is."

"Spell it for me."

"A-L-B-E-R-T-S-O-N-S."

"OK, stay there. I'll be right there to get you." Rick picked him up on the corner one stop past his regular disembarking point. Rick asked Sean, "Why didn't you get off at the right stop?"

"Because I was dancing."

Oh yes, we have our priorities.

Off Campus

Do not follow where the path may lead. Go instead where there is no path and leave a trail. —Ralph Waldo Emerson

The day before school of Sean's junior year he looked at me and just said, "Off campus."

I had no idea what he was talking about, so I asked him what he meant by "Off Campus."

He responded, "For lunch." Oh boy, juniors got to leave the school campus for lunch.

During Sean's sophomore year he had frequently been late to class after snack and lunch. I started to bargain with him, "If you can be on time to class after snack and lunch for the next week, then *next* Friday you can go off campus." He agreed, but he had no intention of sticking to the agreement.

The next day he called me before the lunch bell rang. "Mom, can I go off campus?"

"No. Remember, if you are on time every day for lunch and snack, then *next Friday* you can go off campus."

"I'm going anyway." The bell was ringing as he shouted that into the phone, and then he hung up on me.

His aide called next. "He's leaving the campus! He's leaving the campus!"

I told her to just let him go. "I'll fix him tomorrow, and I'll send him with a lunch and no money. Let me know via the communication notebook if he makes it back on time." He did make it back to class on time after lunch. But he had been late to the class after snack already that day, so he knew he wouldn't be getting off campus for a long time with the "earning" rule.

I packed a lunch and sent it with him the next day—and the stinker took his homemade lunch off campus to the McDonald's across the street from the school and ate it there.

Later in the year I found out he was spending his whole $20 weekly lunch budget on Monday and buying food for all of his friends. Then he would have to take his lunch the rest of the week because he had spent all of his money. He only did that a few times, but our philosophy is that it's his money, he can be stupid with it and learn the natural consequence of being broke that goes with that. Lots of people are stupid with money, so why should the expectation be that he be smarter than the rest of the world?

Proud AND Pissed

Nothing in the world can take the place of persistence. Talent will not; nothing is more common than unsuccessful men with talent. Genius will not; unrewarded genius is almost a proverb. Education alone will not; the world is full of educated derelicts. Persistence and determination alone are omnipotent. The slogan "press on" has solved and always will solve the problems of the human race.—John Calvin Coolidge

In Sean's junior year, he was becoming more and more independent. He had his cell phone and was supposed to call us every time he changed locations. One Friday afternoon, he decided to go to the park across the street from our house to play basketball. My instructions were for him to come home at 5:00, shower, then we were all going to go to the high school football game. At 5:00, I called to remind him he needed to be heading home—but he didn't answer. That was a clue he was not following my instructions. I walked across the street to the park to get him and discovered the basketball court had been resurfaced and he had not been able to play there. He was nowhere to be seen. I called, and called him, and kept ending up in his voice mail. I went home, got in the car, and started looking for him. Rick stayed home in case he called the house phone. As I saw neighbors, I told them to call me if they saw him. They jumped in their cars and began searching too. It was almost 6:00, getting dark, and I was about to call the police when one neighbor called, "I just saw him get on the bus. I tried to get to him, but he was on it before I could reach him. It's the bus heading toward the high school."

He still was not answering his phone and the pending punishments were reeling in my head. I tried to catch up with the bus, to no avail. I was just arriving at the high school when Rick called me. "Sean just called. He said, 'I'm at the school,' then he just hung up on me."

I parked in the high school parking lot and went to the entrance of the football stadium and waited— ready to snatch him up, ground him, and take him home—but he never entered.

A family friend exited the stadium to meet up with somebody and told me he saw Sean sitting in the stands at the football game holding his basketball.

Rick came in his car and when he arrived we went into the stadium, and there Sean was sitting with a friend—and his basketball. (Doesn't everybody bring a basketball to a football game?) We just looked at him, didn't say a word and let him stew on what his consequence would be.

On one hand I was so proud that he had figured out how to get *to* the school, show his student ID to get a ticket, go into the stadium, and complete all of those steps completely on his own. But at the same time, I was so PISSED that he didn't tell me where he was going. That was when I realized he has learned well from me—it's easier to gain forgiveness than permission.

When we drove home that night I informed Sean his video games would be confiscated for the whole weekend. He was disappointed but accepted the consequence to his decision to not answer his phone.

Laundry Lessons

Nobody who says, "I told you so" has ever been, or will ever be, a hero. —Ursula K. Le Guin

One Saturday in Sean's junior year he brought down his laundry basket, and I noticed there wasn't much in it. I had been working a lot that week and leaving early for work each day before he went to school—and Rick never paid attention to Sean's clothing choices. There were two pairs of jeans, three shirts, and *one* pair of underwear in the basket.

I asked him, "Where's the rest of your clothes?"

He said, "That's it."

"Where's your underwear?"

"That's it."

"You wore the *same underwear* every day this week? And only two pairs of pants and three shirts? Gross. Why?"

"I don't have to do a lot of laundry now."

Well, on one hand, that's good problem-solving skills; on the other hand, that's gross. I had to start paying attention and making sure he put on clean clothes. I should have added "different clothes every day" to the chore checklist.

Driving

Never lend your car to anyone to whom you have given birth.— *Erma Bombeck*

As any high school age teen desires, Sean also wanted to learn to drive. Since there is no way Sean will listen to or accept the word "no," I decided to allow him to fail out of driver's education. I signed him up for the "Traffic" class his senior year. "Traffic" was the classroom portion of the driver's education class. The class description read: "The integration of both classroom and laboratory experiences. Students learn the safe operation of the vehicle, the effects of alcohol and other chemicals on driver performance, rules of the road, and positive attitudes when driving within the highway transportation system."

We told Sean he had to take the class and pass two tests, both the learner's permit class and the driver's test, before he could drive. That didn't deter him. The traffic teacher had been his regular education PE teacher, and he accepted Sean into his class. The first 5 days of class they took all five of the state's Beginning Driver's Permit tests. Very few students in the class passed the tests. The point the teacher was making to them is that they needed to study for the tests.

I asked that they *NOT* provide the same accommodations that the state allows—which includes *READING* the questions to the test taker and allowing verbal answers. I didn't want Sean to pass the test. I don't think his reflexes are quick enough to drive and to react fast enough if somebody pulled in front of him or walked in front of his car. But I was not going to discourage him and tell him no. I wanted him to try to come to the same conclusion on his own. He worked hard in the class, but he couldn't pass any of the beginner's permit tests at the end of the semester, when all of his classmates did pass the tests.

When the class was over he said, "I don't need to drive, I can take the bus." We haven't heard much about driving from him since.

There are a lot of advances being made in automation with cars. At this time I do expect Sean will be able to drive one day in a car that has sensors and will stop automatically, or slow itself in traffic. Google has a prototype car that allows you to program the address of your destination, then sit back and relax as the car automatically transports you to the destination. With GPS providing step-by-step instructions on where to turn and sensors to assure me he won't be slamming into other cars—or worse, a pedestrian—I believe even in a busy traffic area that eventually Sean can achieve this goal. The biggest obstacle will be if we can afford the car with all those bells and whistles on it.

ATM Card

I've just got one last thing. I urge all of you, all of you to enjoy your life, the precious moments you have. To spend each day with some laughter and some thought to get your emotions going. — Jim Vlavano

For Sean's sixteenth birthday we went to the DMV and got his California ID card, then went to set up his first bank account. The bank had a student account that was fee-free, and I was able to have access via my account to monitor Sean's use. While Sean could deposit his money and withdraw it from the account through the ATM, I didn't think he should take the ATM card to school. You never know when somebody might try to shake you down if you have too much access to cash.

Toward the end of his junior year, unbeknownst to me, Sean went into my purse and took his ATM card with him to school. I received a phone call from his fifth-period teacher, who said, "Somehow Sean has a credit card and went to McDonald's at lunch and bought $60 worth of burgers. He brought them to fifth period, and he's feeding my class."

I didn't know what to say. "That must be his ATM card." I immediately checked my purse and sure enough, no ATM card. "Thanks for letting me know. I'll talk to him when he gets home."

I knew he only had $50 in the account so I immediately ran to the bank and deposited $20 so there wouldn't be an overdraft charge. After school that day he had his karate class and was supposed to come straight home. When he didn't show up on time I called him, and like he always did when he was doing something inappropriate, he didn't answer his phone. So, I went to Taco Bell looking for him.

Outside the entrance to Taco Bell I found a grocery cart with Sean's backpack in it . . . some grocery bags full of food, and a melting cup of rainbow sherbet that was purchased at the drugstore's ice cream counter—but no Sean. I went into Taco Bell, and there he was with *FOUR* bags of bean burritos (there were 20 burritos) and two huge cups of soda. He was alone, but for some reason had purchased two huge sodas. He was putting the lids on the sodas when he saw me. I wasn't even sure what to say. My son was off the grid, he had lost it. He was on a spree.

All of the Taco Bell employees knew Sean because he was there almost every day. The man working behind the counter said, "I'm a little worried, he has like $200 in his pocket."

I was fuming. "Show me your money." He pulled a huge wad of cash out of his front pocket, and I took it, "Where did you get this?"

Proudly, with his chest puffed out, he said, "The ATM machine." I called Rick to pick him up and take him to karate. I loaded the groceries into the car, and I immediately went to the bank to deposit the cash Sean had withdrawn.

I asked the teller how he was able to overdraw so much. Including all of his purchases and the ATM withdrawal of $200 he had withdrawn almost $350. This was in addition to the $60 in burgers. Turned out the student account included overdraft protection—I cancelled the overdraft protection immediately so any further overdrawn purchases would be declined whenever he went one penny over the account balance. I had to transfer money from my account to cover the additional overdraft, and the teller was nice enough to cancel out the overdraft charges.

Then I took the groceries home and put them away. I was amazed. The items were almost exactly what we purchased every week. Rick had been taking Sean to the grocery store each week and apparently he had been paying attention, except he had twice as much of everything that we usually purchased, and, of course, we already had stocked our groceries for that week.

Two packages of quartered chickens, 2 gallons of milk, there were enough flour tortillas to feed a family of 10 people for a month. The only things he purchased that were not on our regular list were Pop Tarts and 2 gallons of rainbow sherbet—I guess he got the cup of sherbet because he couldn't wait to get home to eat some of the gallons?

I looked inside his backpack. He also had purchased a video game. So his spree consisted of McDonald's, Game Stop, Ralph's Grocery, Rite Aid Drugs, Bank of America for the ATM, and Taco Bell. And it wasn't even 4:00 when I caught up to him. I was so upset. What a failure I was as a parent. I thought we had instilled responsible spending habits.

When he got home from karate we sat down for a family meeting. I asked him why he bought the burgers for the class. At age 16 he still had a hard time answering "why" questions. But this time he had no problem answering. "Samantha."

Of course. He was trying to impress a girl.

From that day forward, he thought he was Mr. Big Bucks. He received so much positive reinforcement from his classmates for buying the burgers that now he always wants to buy meals for his friends—even if there's 10 of them. The endorphin rush of successfully purchasing the rest of the items, and then cashing in with $200 out of the ATM skewed his thinking forever. The boy who saved for 6 months to buy an Xbox 360 was gone. We still can't trust him with more money than what he needs for the day; he will spend every dime. And my lesson was that not everything we teach is perfect or permanent.

We have tried various budgeting tools, even purchased a coupon folder and labeled each pocket with the names of the days of the week, and put his money for each day into the pockets. He still will take all of the money out on Monday and be broke by the end of the day. Sometimes he will even get a haircut to use up the money—even when he just had a haircut the previous week. We have to dole out his money each day with a list of what he is to use it for so he doesn't spend everything before noon. Hopefully one day he will return to the boy who saved for 6 months for an Xbox 360.

Sean Waits for No One

Golf without bunkers and hazards would be tame and monotonous. So would life. — B. C. Forbes

During the summer between Sean's junior and senior year we were taking a 1-week vacation in Palm Desert at a Time Share Resort. Sean was instructed to stay in the room while we went to a sales presentation, with the promise that he and Dad would play golf when we returned. We ended up taking too long, (according to Sean's standards), and Rick decided to call him to give him our ETA. Here's how the conversation went.

"Hi Sean, we're almost done. I'll be there in about 20 minutes."

"OK, Dad, I'm on the golf course."

"Where are you?"

"I'm on the first tee."

"How did you get there?"

"I drove there. Wait, talk to *this guy*." Sean said to *the guy*, "This is my dad."

The guy answered, "Hello?"

Rick said, "Who is this, and where is Sean?"

The guy said, "I'm the Starter and was showing Sean to the first tee." Rick told him to hold Sean there, not to let him go. Thankfully the presentation center for the time share resort was near the first tee. Rick quickly ran out to the first tee, and there was Sean, sitting in a golf cart, his clubs perfectly strapped to the cart. The Starter was in his own cart.

Rick talked to the Starter and asked what had happened and why Sean was driving a golf cart. We had to do some forensic work, but after everything was revealed, here's how Sean did it:

Sean had left our room with his golf clubs and started walking toward the Pro Shop—about a 1-mile walk in 115 degrees of desert heat. The resort's shuttle bus came by and asked if he wanted a ride and Sean told the driver, "Yes, take me to golf." The shuttle dropped him at the Pro Shop.

Sean had gone inside, approached the counter, and said, "I want to play golf." The pro behind the counter asked him how he wanted to pay and he responded, "Put it on my room." He gave them our room number and showed them his key card, and then signed for a round of golf to be billed to our room. They asked to see his driver's license, and Sean pulled out his wallet and showed them his California State ID, which looks like a driver's license, so they gave him a cart.

The Pro said Sean carried his clubs out, put them on the back of the cart, and strapped them in. He appeared to know what he was doing. Then he asked Sean if he knew where the first tee was, and he responded, "Nope."

So the Pro asked the Starter to show Sean where to go. The Starter got into his cart and said, "Follow me." Sean got into *his own cart and drove out* to the first tee following the Starter—and that's when Rick had called.

Rick arranged to have the round of golf and the cart removed from our bill. He did take Sean to the driving range, but it was too hot to play a round of golf at noon in August in Palm Desert.

Were we mad at Sean? No. We were pretty proud that he was able to do this all by himself—including driving the cart. We're also thankful that Rick called and found Sean before he started on 18 holes, because he would have played all 18 holes before stopping. We were also glad the Pro Shop didn't think there was anything strange about somebody with Down syndrome charging a round of golf on their room. Sean acted confident, and they said he seemed to know what he was doing, so they didn't question anything about it. And that's the way it should be.

Baptism

Baptism separates the tire kickers from the car buyers. — Max Lucado

Sean had been volunteering at the children's ministry for a couple of years and had seen many people get baptized between church services. It was summer, and we were at a pool party at a friend's house, who happens to be a pastor at our church. Sean walked up to him and said, "Brett, will you baptize me?"

He responded, "Now? We can do it in the pool."

But Sean had another plan. He said, "Nope, on my birthday." So we began preparations for Sean's seventeenth birthday baptism.

Brett had a great idea . . . Why not baptize some of Sean's friends at the same time? So we sent out an e-mail and four of Sean's friends decided to join him. We had over 100 friends come to witness the event. Sean was determined he wanted to be baptized last. Brett had the microphone and was interviewing each young man as they were about to go into the water.

When Sean's turn came, Brett said, "They say that every time somebody gets baptized that the angels in heaven rejoice. What do you think the angels sound like today?"

Sean took the microphone out of Brett's hand and began to sing, "Take me out to the ball game . . ." Holding up his arms he yelled, "Come on. Everybody sing along!"

The whole group began to sing, "Root-Root-Root for the Angels . . . And it's one, two, three strikes you're out at the old ball game."

I realized I had not done a very good job explaining the angels in heaven to Sean. He knew about Jesus, God, and the Holy Spirit, but the "Angels" he was thinking of were not the ones in heaven.

Brett just thought, "That's Sean," and didn't understand why he sang the Seventh Inning Stretch song, but most everybody else understood Sean was thinking of his favorite baseball team—the Los Angeles Angels of Anaheim.

Progress Is Constant

"Fear Not" is in the Bible 365 times. One for every day of the year.
—Rick Warren

In order to achieve lifelong independence, Sean has to constantly make progress. Sean has no problem letting people do things for him. At age 18 we were out to dinner and he asked us to cut his chicken for him—he is perfectly capable of cutting his own food—but he also likes to be waited on too. We kindly told him that if he was unable to cut his own food, he should have ordered something else. So he picked up the knife in his right hand, fork in his left, and proceeded to properly cut his food—as he was taught several years ago.

We love to vacation and are fortunate enough to have a great Time Share Plan that allows us at least 2 weeks a year in luxury resorts. We usually get 2-bedroom time shares, and Sean has his own room, but sometimes we end up with a one-bedroom model and he has to sleep on a sofa sleeper. We have taught him how to open the sofa sleepers and make his bed. Now, completely unprompted, he will take the cushions off the sofa, stack them neatly next to it, then pull out the sofa sleeper, cheering himself as he goes with the success of creating his bed for the night. Every day for the next 7 days he will put his sofa back together in the morning, and open it back up at night. This frequent repetition makes the difference in the speed of learning for Sean.

The summer before his senior year Flag Football practices had started. A conversation I had with another mom during a Friday football practice still lingers in my mind. She asked me, "What is Sean doing the rest of this summer?"

"Well, since summer school is over and surf camp is over and we're heading out of town tomorrow he has just been home the last 2 weeks, bored and entertaining himself with TV, Wii, and creating party invitations on the computer and going around the neighborhood and inviting everybody to 'imaginary' parties at our house. Some days he walks to Taco Bell for lunch or walks to the pool, but it's been hot and the pool is a mile away and he doesn't like to walk that far in the heat."

Her teeth were dropping out of her mouth. "You leave him alone?"

My response, "Yes, he's not going to live with me forever, so he's got to be independent."

I know that there are many teens and adults with disabilities who are unable to safely be left home by themselves. But I also know many who are capable, but their families are too fearful to even try. Everybody has to do what is in their comfort zone. I had to leave any comfort zone I had to help Sean be as independent as possible for his future safety and independence.

Define Free

Easy come. Easy go. —*American Proverb*

Sean doesn't get much mail, but when he does, it's a huge deal to him. One day he got a solicitation from *Sports Illustrated* magazine stating he would get a "free" jacket if he subscribed to the magazine . . . I decided to try to use this as a "teaching moment." He read the letter. "MOM. It says, 'YOURS FREE.' It's a coat, and it's free."

I said, "Really? What else does it say?" I had to point to the "smaller print" below.

He read, "Sports . . . something that starts with an 'I' for $28."

I said, "It says, 'Illustrated.' That's a magazine about sports."

"Cool, I like sports."

"How much does the magazine cost?"

"$28."

"Do you have to pay for the magazine to get the coat?"

"Yeah . . ."

"So, is it still 'free'?"

"No. That is *MEAN*. I thought it was free. I don't like this." Then into the trash it went.

Whew, I could see him being a huge target for every direct mail campaign. Hopefully, he remembers this lesson.

Social Life

A healthy social life is found only when in the mirror of each soul the whole community finds its reflection, and when in the whole community the virtue of each one is living. — Rudolf Steiner

We all need a rich social life. As Sean gets older I see more and more of his friends who hit their early 20s and become depressed. They aren't able to verbalize that they feel sad, and they may not even know why they feel sad, but the regression that comes with the depression is devastating. I can't stress enough how critical it is to facilitate friendships and activities for our kids to keep them happy and active.

When Inclusion Becomes Exclusion

The most imperfect model is the pursuit of perfection. — Byrd Baggett

It was a journey to Sean's senior year of high school—some of it amazing, and some, sadly, less than amazing.

Even though the law provides for inclusive education, you cannot legislate attitudes, and that includes not just the educators but also other parents' attitudes.

One issue that reared its ugly head in the last 2 years of high school is *disability prejudice* WITHIN *the disability community.* Ann Turnbull calls it disability elitism.

Parents who chose not to include their children in regular education, for a host of reasons, found themselves in a happy community of people who have created their friendships apart from those who elected inclusive education—to the point of EXCLUDING the teens that had been fully included.

And the sad reality occurred where the *typical* students who so readily accepted our kids in elementary school—I almost went broke buying gifts for all the birthday parties Sean was invited to—now have their own lives and are very nice, but rarely called and invited Sean to any parties, sports events . . . well—any place at all.

And then there was Sean's *attitude* toward other people who have disabilities. One of the ulterior motives behind inclusion (other than an education and appropriate social skills) is to sensitize typical students to not be afraid of people with disabilities. To teach them, by daily exposure, that we are all more alike than different. But to that end, our students who HAVE the disabilities also are not exposed to other people with disabilities—when the other parents choose a segregated education for their children. Thus, this conversation that occurred with Sean on the way to his first Red Carpet Ball—the formal dance that the Down Syndrome Association of Orange County holds each February:

"Mom, is everybody there going to have Down syndrome?"

"Well, most everybody. They can bring a date who could have a different disability or no disability, but you have to have Down syndrome to even buy a ticket. Why?"

He thought for a minute, then said, "Because my Down syndrome is different than theirs." He was unable to verbalize *what* was different between *his* and *their* Down syndrome—but it's probably a lot like me—when I see someone my same age and I think, *My wrinkles aren't THAT bad . . . Are they?* Denial is a lovely thing.

Sean was 15 when that conversation happened, and I recognized then that I needed to do some *disability immersion* or he was going to be one lonely boy. Or worse, become fearful of people with disabilities.

So, we attended every disability event possible and did fun things with friends who were disabled and even started a social club named Cool Club, with 16 teens that have disabilities.

I realized this was not an isolated issue when Sean began dating another young woman who has also been fully included. She would pull me aside and tell me about another boy she liked *better* than Sean on almost every date—this boy did not have Down syndrome, and also had no interest in her. But just like Sean, she saw her Down syndrome as *different,* and she ultimately decided she did not want a boyfriend with Down syndrome and broke up with Sean.

Sean especially had a strong aversion to people in wheelchairs. He needed a volunteer job, so we approached the person in charge of our disabilities ministry at our church, and she agreed to allow Sean to volunteer in the Under Age 10 Special Stars Sunday School Class.

The first Sunday there were four boys in wheelchairs. After church I was quizzing Sean how the morning went. He said, "Mom, they creep me out." So we had an opportunity to talk about how they were just like him, but they used wheels instead of feet.

It took a few months, but the proof that he was desensitized came when some volunteers for the U.S. Adapted Recreation Center in Big Bear, California, were teaching waterskiing and jet skiing to people with both intellectual and physical disabilities. There was a woman in a wheelchair with her ambulatory husband. Sean was fascinated by them. He sat on the ground in front of her wheelchair for about 30 minutes having a great conversation—till I heard him start getting too personal. He asked, "Are you two married? For how long? How did you meet?" I was getting concerned that he was about to ask them if they had sex . . . and how when in his mind she must always be in a chair . . . so I joined in the conversation and redirected the trajectory. But he was completely comfortable, probably *too* comfortable, and I realized the disability immersion program I had instituted a year earlier had been effective.

So, heads-up when you fully include your kids and nobody else does. Remember to supplement with outside activities involving peers who also have disabilities. And for those of you who did not choose inclusion? Can we play?

Cool Club

I wrote the following article for the National Down Syndrome Congress newsletter. I presented Cool Club to two conferences, encouraging parents to start one in their area.

Teens and Adults with Intellectual Disabilities Don't Need to Be Socially Isolated
By Sandra McElwee, Rancho Santa Margarita, California

With no social activities on the calendar and a long summer looming ahead, an idea was hatched. Dreading the inevitable boredom, 16 teens and their parents banded together to create something new—Cool Club. The Cool Club's mission is to provide a safe, fun environment where members are encouraged to develop trusting friendships, learn appropriate social and communication skills, and promote tolerance and patience between members and their families. One year later, Cool Club is a great success.

How it works
The concept is pretty simple. Most teenagers like to socialize with friends, and teens with intellectual disabilities (ID) are no different. But teens with ID may have less opportunity to hang out with peers without some assistance in planning and executing social gatherings. With Cool Club, families take 1 weekend to plan an evening activity for a group of teens. Being responsible for 1 weekend means 15 more

weeks of fun planned by other parents. Even the busiest parents could muster up three times a year. So, two moms quickly set up a calendar and each family picked a weekend to host the group.

The moms also put together some rules about communication, supervision, and basic requirements that all families agreed to follow.

Since it was summer, there were a lot of pool parties and bowling was a hit too. We quickly learned our group didn't like to sit quietly and watch a movie at the theater. They want to socialize with each other, laugh loudly, and high-five each other without disturbing other moviegoers. So, a movie in someone's home is better. Our teens like to do anything that other teens do—play miniature golf, hang out at the mall, eat at Benihana and other restaurants with an entertaining theme, and watch plays and sporting events.

Each week, the host family e-mails all club members with the day and date of the event (Friday or Saturday), location, including address and pertinent phone numbers, time to arrive and pick up, what the event will entail (bowling, party, swimming, etc.), and any special instructions, such as the amount of money needed, food for potlucks, etc. There must be a minimum of one man and one woman at every event, so the single moms and dads request another parent to help when it's their turn to host.

While their teens are at Cool Club, parents enjoy date nights or just have weekend time alone. This isn't a "babysitting" co-op, however. Parents can't leave siblings to potentially double the number of teens. The hosts, though, can have all of their other children there to help out. If a planned activity needs additional supervision, that information is included in the e-mail and another set of parents volunteer to help.

The format has been very manageable. Out of 16 teens, attendance averages eight to 10 per activity. Attendance is not required for every activity and several members have single parents and are not available every weekend. Our teens attend five different high schools. Many have participated on the same sports teams since they were children and some know each other from school. Several have a common friend in the group, but most are new friends. None had frequent social opportunities before Cool Club was founded and new friendships have bloomed.

All are welcome

We do not tolerate intolerance. Every teen in Cool Club has had an issue at some point in their lives. To accept everybody, no matter what, is what we look for in our communities, so we want to be the models of that acceptance. *Everybody* deserves the opportunity to have friends and fun, so everyone is welcome and accepted. We have a few members with behavioral issues, such as eloping or hitting. Parents know if their teen fits that description. If so, the teen is welcome to come with a parent in attendance. One young woman used to need her parents' presence. But now that she knows what is expected of her, she rises to the occasion and is able to come solo. She is awesome.

What is the hardest part of Cool Club? Well, the original group had a couple of unreliable parents. When it was their week to host, they dropped their teens out of the group in lieu of hosting. All of the teens were bummed to have a weekend with nothing planned for them to do. For the rest of the parents, it was a reminder of what life was like *before* Cool Club. We are more dedicated than ever to continue.

Building on success

It's time for some new Cool Clubs to form. As other parents have found out about our Cool Club they've begged to have their teens join. We are committed to keeping the group size manageable, so we're helping other parents to start their own Cool Clubs.

The most difficult part of forming a new Cool Club is finding potential members who are interested in social activities. While everyone knows at least one other person with a disability, word of mouth only works to a certain extent. To find a larger group of prospective members I approached a local organization that serves clients with a range of disabilities, which allowed me to do a Cool Club presentation to clients and families. They advertised the event through e-mail blasts forwarded around the county. I shared how our club started, and then I split them into groups by age—high school, transition age—and adult—and more Cool Clubs were formed. Ask your local DS association, school district's special education department, transition programs, Parent to Parent, or other organizations that serve clients with ID to help spread the word too.

Because adults with ID also need the same social opportunities, I plan on starting some adult groups. I'd suggest limiting the group to about 12 since adults may have fewer social opportunities than teens and will attend every week.

It's been almost a year now, and I've planned three (manageable) events. My son hates to miss a Cool Club activity, and every Friday his questions start—*When is Cool Club? Who is doing it? What are we doing?* Parents find the teens are starting to plan (okay, dictate) their own activities and now our job is to follow through with the details.

As I finalize this book, Cool Club has been going on for 4 years, and there is no end in sight. Teens and adults with no social opportunities become depressed, and depression creates behaviors that nobody should have to endure.

Diploma or Certificate of Completion?

Some quit due to slow progress, never grasping the fact that slow progress is progress.—Unknown

We weighed the pros and cons of getting a diploma for quite a while. Finally we decided not to pursue a diploma for three reasons.

1. Sean was not that interested in achieving one, and it would have taken a lot of hard work for him to complete all the credits he needed to graduate.
2. The State CAHSEE (California High School Exit Examination). He could have probably passed the math portion with hard work but would have never been able to write the essay portion of the English exam.
3. We were told repeatedly that he would be exited from the school district if he achieved a diploma and would not be able to attend the district's transition program. And I was told repeatedly by every person I asked, from the Regional Center, the school district, education advocates— everybody—that he would not have any support or access to any programs between graduation and age 22 if he received a diploma.

One year after Sean completed high school, the state of California suspended the CAHSEE for students with special educational needs.

They accepted the required class credits toward a diploma. Then another year later, I found out if Sean *had* received a diploma, that he could have accessed the Regional Center's (Department of Developmental Disabilities) funding for a Day Program, allowing him to have community college support, a real paying job with a job coach and more. Check your state's rules and know they can, and do, change. In hindsight, we should have continued pursing the diploma and the decision could have been made a week before school ended whether Sean would have received a certificate of completion or diploma. (You will read later in this story that I was misinformed by everyone and Sean could have accessed a Day Program earlier.)

Transition IEP

A lot of people resist transition and therefore never allow themselves to enjoy who they are. Embrace the change, no matter what it is; once you do, you can learn about the new world you're in and take advantage of it. — Nikki Giovanni

At the end of Sean's senior year we attended his IEP to transition into our school district's transition program. Sean wanted to present a PowerPoint presentation to the transition team, and with my help and the help of his case carrier he created a nice one that clearly described his goals and what he wanted to accomplish in his transition program.

I brought my laptop and projector from work, he stood up at the front of the room, and delivered the presentation, advancing the slides by himself, like he had practiced with his teacher. We included the text on each slide so they could read his words as he spoke them in case they couldn't understand his articulation. After he read each slide he looked at each person in the room before moving to the next one. It was a great delivery.

His presentation began with an introduction of his diagnosis and needs, then his current abilities—the ones he thought they should know about, then *his* goals for *his* future.

I have Down syndrome
- It's an explanation—not an excuse

- I am deaf in my right ear
- I have to sit close to the person speaking
- Sometimes it's hard to understand my speech; just ask me to say it again
- I don't like to write
- I can read OK
- I am a visual learner

I have lots of friends (photo of him at his Winter Formal with a group in front of the limo)

I volunteer (photos of him as Santa's elf, the Sunday school class he volunteers in, and leading the Buddy Walk for our local Down Syndrome Association)

I am a good athlete (photos of him playing football, surfing, bowling, golf, karate, and baseball)

I am the favorite assistant of the varsity baseball team (photo of him playing the music between innings)

I am in High Rollers, Best Buddies, and Cool Club (photos of him at each club)

I started the Glee Fan Club (photo of him on club Rush Day)

My girlfriend is on the TV show *Glee,* and she is making me famous (two articles he was in because of her)

Here Are My Goals:

I have a bank account and an ATM card, but I need a budget (photo of him at the ATM machine)

I want my driver's license (photo of him driving a go-cart with his girlfriend next to him)

I want to travel (map of the U.S. marked with places he has already been)

I want my own house

I Know How To:
- Clean house
- Do dishes
- Do laundry
- Care for myself
- Entertain myself

I want to get married (photo of him with his girlfriend)

I want six-pack abs like Sam Evans on *Glee* (photo of Sam Evans with his shirt off)

I want to be an usher at Angel Stadium (photo of the stadium and an usher)

I want to work at Taco Bell (picture of Taco Bell)

I want to work at Boomers (photo of him at Boomers)
- Clean up
- Vacuum
- Start the rides
- Restock supplies

I am a hard worker
- But I know that I don't like working in a clothing store
- I already know how to ride the (Orange County Transit Authority) bus
- I'm friendly

I want to take classes at Saddleback Community College
- Memory and attention skills
- Phonetic structure for reading and spelling
- American Sign Language 1
- Lip reading and hearing conservation
- Drama classes
- Acting
- Bowling
- Introduction to Jazz dancing

- Contemporary meals
- Adapted personalized fitness
- Adapted outdoor education and recreation
- Basketball
- Beginning bowling
- Beginning golf
- Beginning tennis

Can you support my goals?

Sean's future teacher was speechless. She had never had a student present their goals to her. She proceeded to present Sean with canned goals that everyone in her class would receive. It was apparent to me that there would be no individualization and everybody would be doing the same thing in the classes. I was very proud of Sean for leading the meeting and making his wishes known so adeptly.

Summer after Graduation

Stupid risks make life worth living. — *Homer Simpson*

Sean graduated from high school and his transition program didn't begin until September. (Our neighboring district's programs began a week after graduation.) Most of his peers who would be attending the program attended high school summer school classes, but Sean was *done* with school and wanted nothing to do with that option. We pieced the summer together to make it as interesting as possible for him.

In July he attended the inaugural *College Bound* program that was held in San Diego. The 12 students who attended stayed in dorm rooms at Point Loma Nazarene University. It introduced the attendees to the real flavor of college life. Each day they had speakers teaching them about the qualities that college students need: organization, cooperation, good problem-solving skills, and a willingness to work.

We attended the graduation ceremony on Friday night and noticed Sean was quite popular among the students. Before the ceremony one mother told us that she had been talking to her son on the phone earlier in the week when he abruptly hung up on her saying, "I've got to go—there's a party in Sean's room."

They showed a slide show of the week, and in every photo that was in a classroom, Sean was asleep. In every group shot when they were touring the campus, eating in the cafeteria, or on other outings he was making the hand gesture from the band KISS, "The Sign of the

Horns," complete with the Gene Simmons's tongue sticking out. (All that therapy to keep the tongue in his mouth and he's displaying it on purpose?) Where he learned that, I cannot tell you. That's one thing about independence, you can't know everything, and since I am a control freak that's hard for me.

As the director of the program described their week she emphasized that the students did truly experience a *real* college experience. Complete with the dorm room parties that keep the serious students up all night. Sean was the instigator of the dorm room parties, playing his music at the maximum volume level on his iPod's built-in speakers, while serving bottled water and the snacks we had supplied him with for the week.

He was home for a week, then went to Young Life's Summer Camp, always a high point in the summer. One more boring week home then we went to the National Down Syndrome Congress Convention in San Antonio, Texas. He met a cute girl named Maggie there since his girlfriend had broken up with him, yet again.

We spent a few days with Grandma in Ft. Worth, Texas, afterward.

He then had 3 more boring weeks where he sometimes went to the community center, sometimes went swimming at the community pool, or just stayed home and played video games and watched movies.

Sean had enough of his boring summer and was very was ready when the little yellow bus picked him up the first day for his transition program.

Transition Begins

When you're the only sane person, you look like the only insane person.
—Criss Jami

The first 2 weeks of the transition program they were supposed to "Bus Train" everyone on how to take the public OCTA (Orange County Transit Authority) bus round-trip from home to the transition program, then the little yellow bus would be discontinued. But a month later, the bus was still coming for Sean, so I contacted his teacher. She explained that because he had not attended the Special Day Class in high school they were waiting to train him last. "Since he isn't used to riding the bus it is going to take him longer than it is taking for the students who are used to riding the bus."

"I don't think that is true because Sean took the bus independently for the past 2 years. The SDC class always had an aide or teacher with them, and Sean didn't."

She was surprised, and I realized Sean was being stereotyped. Once they started his training, they only had to show Sean twice how to get to the transition program. It was over an hour one way because of the bus schedules, and he had to change buses once. It was truly a 20-minute drive if I drove him, but taking the bus was part of the program.

They then commenced to show the students how to go everywhere in Orange County. Bowling alleys, movie theatres, many different beaches, every mall in the county, Disneyland, and more. The thing that was hard about this was once he knew how to get every-where Sean would just go—and I would have no idea *where* he was.

Sean turned 18, and he applied for SSI. By Christmas, he started receiving checks. He decided that he didn't have to do chores to earn money any more now that he had his own money. I did limit the amount he could have access to at any one time, but if he decided he wanted more money he started getting into my purse and helping himself to the dollars in my wallet. Or worse, take his ATM card and go on a spree.

Consequences for an 18-year-old are tough. I still took his iPod away. That was the most effective consequence. Grounding him from the TV or Wii worked as well. He was in Cool Club, and sometimes, I wouldn't allow him to attend an event. Having him earn rewards instead of giving consequences for punishments were always a big motivator for Sean. But if he fell short of earning the prize then all was lost.

Rick and I would promise him a weekend getaway *if* he was on time to school, cleaned his room, or whatever behavior we were try-ing to change. But when he blew it and didn't go to school on time and didn't experience success, everything went out the window, so immediate rewards, like going to the movies or out to dinner or buy-ing ice cream *today* were much more motivating and effective.

Sean was so bored in his transition program. The class was very slow-paced. On Mondays, they went to the grocery store to buy food that they would cook on Wednesday. Sean's cooking goal on his IEP was the same as the other students' goals, "To find the word 'Microwave' on the package and the number of minutes to cook the item."

Microwaveable meals are the most fattening, sodium-filled, non-nutritious things you can buy in a grocery store. I was very disap-pointed they weren't learning to cook real food. Or even make a sandwich or a salad.

Tuesdays and Thursdays, the students had their "Work Experience" where they went to a variety of "practice jobs" and worked for zero wages.

On Fridays, the whole class, or sometimes all three classes together, would go on CBI—Community-Based Instruction. But CBI consisted of bowling, seeing a movie, or going to one of the gazillion malls in our area, roaming around and having lunch. In my opinion, this was a huge waste of time.

We waited and waited for Sean to be assigned to a work experience. At the beginning of December I e-mailed his teacher and asked her when Sean would begin and what he was scheduled to do. I had this idea in my head that was completely wrong. I assumed that there was a group of existing jobs the program had lined up and each student would try each job for a couple of months, then rotate to try a different one, thus, giving each student a flavor for what each job consisted of, and then they could get an idea of what work they enjoyed and what they didn't like to do.

His teacher responded that Sean was slated to work at a nursing home along with another student who has Down syndrome. She told me that it was a great work site since they *let* the students do any number of jobs there, including serving food, cleaning tables, and working in the kitchen, cleaning toilets, vacuuming, and more. To me, it sounded like torture, but I didn't want to limit Sean's opportunities so we waited.

I called some of my friends in January whose young adults were also in the program and found out they had started working in October. One was at a grocery store, another one at a senior citizen center. Sean and one other student were the only two students with Down syndrome and the only two students who were not working yet. I started fuming.

I called the teacher once again, and she said the nursing home had gone through a renovation and they were still waiting for the manager to give them a start date. Our church had opened a food bank, and I asked if they could work at the food bank as volunteers since they wouldn't be getting paid for their work anyway. They were open to the idea. I called the person in charge of our food bank and set up the meeting for Sean, the other student, and the job coach. In the beginning of February he finally began working.

The transition program included a goal in Sean's IEP that he would make his lunch each day at home and bring it to class. Sean hated making his lunch. He would prefer to buy his lunch any day of the week rather than make it. Every day was the same; he would wait until the last minute to make his lunch, run out of time, and I would have to make it quickly for him. Every morning was a fight and stressful.

In January I told him I wouldn't make his lunch anymore, and if he didn't make it he could just eat when he got home from school.

Sean problem-solved the lunch issue all by himself. In the mornings he would stop by Carl's Jr., which is next door to Taco Bell, and buy his lunch before boarding his bus. He would have bought lunch at Taco Bell, but they weren't open that early. I didn't know he was doing this, and thought he was just choosing to starve because he wasn't taking his lunch. I learned about his morning purchase when his teacher asked me, "Why are you letting Sean bring food from Carl's?" I was floored. He has always had great problem-solving skills.

We had Sean's annual IEP in the spring, and I asked why they didn't make lunch as a part of the class. I had been to a seminar where another transition program also shopped on Mondays, but then they came back to class and made their lunches for the week, filling the refrigerator with their brown bags that they also purchased at the store. They purchased loaves of bread, lunchmeat, fruit and worked on having a balanced diet as part of their assignment of making lunch. But Sean's transition program refused to add that as an IEP goal. They rationalized it was only Monday, Tuesday, and Thursday he needed to bring a lunch since they cooked their microwave dinner on Wednesday and ate out on Friday.

Fitness

The first time I see a jogger smiling, I'll consider it. — Joan Rivers

Sean was still playing some sports, but there were going to be fewer and fewer available as he got older. Special Olympics practices were only once a week, and that wasn't going to be enough to keep him as fit as he was. One of his personal goals that he had set was to have six-pack abs, so we bought him a 2-year membership to 24 Hour Fitness. I was also a member and thought if I had to take Sean, then maybe I would actually go too.

Sean and his friend Mark signed up for 10 personal training sessions together. The trainer taught them how to use the machines, how to set the weights, impressed on them that it was important to warm up on a bike or treadmill first, and taught them how to stretch after their workout. Sean loved learning all the machines, and he was on his way to staying fit.

After Sean completed the training sessions and learned how to use the machines he would go to the gym by himself. I would call him after school looking for him, and he would tell me he was at the gym. He figured out the bus route all by himself how to get there and back.

Then one day he came home and refused to take a shower. He told me he had showered at the gym. They have soap, and he did smell good, but I don't think Sean had a towel, other than his hand towel-sized workout towel to dry off with.

He started packing a towel, his deodorant, and clean clothes in his backpack and went to 24 Hour Fitness many days after his transition program. He worked out and showered there, then came home all clean and starving for dinner.

Community College

Every year, many, many stupid people graduate from college. And if they can do it, so can you. — John Green

During the spring IEP, after almost a full school year in the transition program, we pressed them for community college support again. They stood their ground and said they would not be supporting students at the local community college. I explained that Sean had been taking classes already, without support.

The first semester he took Beginning Golf on Monday night. Sean had been very anxious about another new school. (He had a very bad experience in intermediate school and the beginning of high school.) To alleviate his anxiety, Rick and I both went with him. The class was on the driving range on the campus, so it wasn't weird that we were there. We were sitting on a bench watching the class when the golf coach came over and introduced himself. He then proceeded to tell us his 40-year-old son also has Down syndrome. We knew Sean would do great in the class, and he made an "A."

The other class he wanted was Acting 1. That class was on Saturday mornings. I took Sean the first day to show him where the class was, and as we approached the room another student was standing outside and said, "Hi, Sean." I asked, "How do you know Sean?" "I just graduated from high school with him last year. I've known Sean all 4 years." BINGO. Just the person I was looking for. I introduced myself and asked this handsome young man if he would be interested in acting as Sean's aide in class, and since he lived near us, driving him to and from class each Saturday.

I paid him minimum wage from the time he picked Sean up in the morning until he dropped him back at home. The student aide reported the homework assignments to us each week, and we would help Sean prepare for the next week. It was a pretty easy class, a lot of improvisation, so there wasn't a lot of preparation—until the final assignment. Sean and his student-aide were to perform a two-person scene. I volunteered to find the scene for them, and Sean approved the selection.

I printed out their scripts and highlighted Sean's lines for him. The student aide was supposed to come over to rehearse, but every time we had it scheduled, he had something come up and couldn't make it. After 2 weeks of missed opportunities they headed to class without one rehearsal. When it came their turn to perform the scene, the student aide mistakenly thought the teacher would let Sean read from their scripts. She forbid it. Her very reasonable argument was they should have been able to memorize that short script within 2 weeks. Unfortunately, the anxiety was too much for Sean. He freaked out and yelled at her. He received an "F" for the entire semester.

That spring semester we enrolled him in Beginning Golf again and Beginning Bowling. He earned an "A" in both classes. The golf class was on Thursday nights, and the bowling class was Mondays and Wednesdays after his transition program. He simply took the bus from his transition program to the bowling alley after school on those days.

During Sean's next IEP I explained that if Sean had had support in the acting class he would not have made an "F." They glossed over it, continued to refuse support, and I told them that Sean would not be at the transition program the following fall on Mondays and Wednesdays because he would be taking community college classes those days.

The way public school funding works in California, the schools get paid based on attendance. It's somewhere in the ballpark of $50 per student per day. If a student doesn't attend one day, the district doesn't get the money for that day. They protested that their program would suffer financially if Sean wasn't there those 2 days. I said, "Well, if you sent an aide with five students in one class, like the two districts that flank ours do, then you wouldn't lose $100 a week on Sean."

Summer Transition Program

I haven't been everywhere, but it's on my list.—Susan Sontag

Cheapest summer camp ever. I was so disappointed that the transition program didn't continue the same curriculum, boring as it was, throughout the summer. I thought Sean should continue working at the food bank and live a normal *adult* life. But the transition program had a different agenda. A few weeks before summer we received a packet that detailed out the summer program.

It was shortened to Tuesday, Wednesday, and Thursday for 4 weeks. Students had to be able to ride the bus independently in order to participate because they had to meet at different locations around the county. The activities ranged from taking the train to San Diego, going to an Angel's baseball game, concerts in the park, the county fair, amusement parks, and much more. It was very fresh and fun, and Sean had a blast playing and learning more places to go on the bus.

The teacher that organized the summer program told her students that they were being "watched" and that only some of them would be allowed to be in her class in the fall because there wasn't enough room for everyone. Sean was stressed out every day. If he thought he was going to be late he would freak out on me. He really wanted to please this teacher and be in her class in the fall. There were some mornings I heard him get up at 3 a.m. and try to leave the house. He was so stressed out about possibly being late that he couldn't even sleep. I had to try to reason with him that the OCTA bus didn't leave that early and assure him that I would make sure he was on time. Then I couldn't go back to sleep.

Birthday Present

Kids need experiences that stretch them, reveal their talents, and develop their shape for ministry. They need challenges where they develop responsibility. One of the most important life skills that all of us have to learn is how to be responsible. — Rick Warren

Sean had wanted an iPhone for quite a while. I had resisted buying him one because his iPod was a perfect motivator. Sean loved his music, and if I needed to give him a consequence, taking his iPod away from him was a perfect consequence, and it always worked as a motivator to gain his compliance. I knew if he had an iPhone he could put his music on it, and I would lose that motivator. And the more independent he was becoming, the less I was able to give him effective consequences.

His nineteenth birthday was approaching and all he wanted was an iPhone. I decided he would get one because of this story.

Over the summer, when the transition program was on break, Sean was home alone and decided to go to visit his friend Ben. Ben's neighborhood had two points of entry, and driving to his house, and we always took the same route. But the bus stopped near the entrance we never traveled and Sean wasn't used to going to Ben's house from that direction.

It was a hot Friday August afternoon. I was heading home and called Sean to remind him to take a shower because he had an event that evening to go to. He answered his cell phone, "Hi, Mom."

I could hear him breathing heavy. "Hi, Sean, what are you doing?"

"I'm at Ben's house."

"What? How did you get there?"

"The bus."

"Really? Let me talk to Ben's mom."

"She's not here."

"So you and Ben are there alone?"

"No, I'm almost there."

Expressive and receptive language deficits made some conversations impossible.

I was a little concerned whether Ben and his mom would even be home, and concerned that Sean needed to learn that it is rude to just pop into someone's house without calling first. Then I was concerned if Ben was home alone, what kind of mischief could they get into unsupervised. They are great friends, and individually, are pretty smart, but when they are together . . . Well, one of my friends said it best: "One boy, half a brain; two boys, no brain."

"Sean, how close are you to their house?"

"I'm on their street, almost there." I was pretty impressed that he had maneuvered so successfully but still wasn't sure he would find their house. I told him to keep talking to me till he got there, and I started driving in that direction. Sean walked and walked, and we talked and talked, and then he said, "It's not here. Ben's house isn't here." I knew he had taken a wrong turn somewhere, then I began to wonder if he was actually *in* Ben's neighborhood at all.

I asked him to go back to the corner and read the street signs. I was still driving and was about 15 minutes away from the neighborhood. He got to the corner and said, "I don't know what it says." There are a lot of streets in our area with Spanish names, and these two were in that category.

"Spell one of them for me."

"C-A-L-L-E F-L-O-R-E-S."

I had pulled into a parking lot and was writing it down as he spelled it. "OK, spell the other one."

"S-A-N-T-O-L-I-N-A."

"OK, just sit down on the sidewalk and wait a minute. I have to put this in my GPS." I entered the cross streets into my GPS and there it was. ONE block in the wrong direction from Ben's house. He had just taken a right when he should have taken a left. He was in the mirror image location of where Ben's house should have been, just one block away.

"OK, Sean, I'm on my way to get you. Stay there. Then I will show you where Ben's house is. You just had one wrong turn."

We talked for a few more minutes, and then he said, "My phone is dying." One more reason for an iPhone. They have great battery life.

I picked Sean up and took him to show him where Ben's house was. Turns out they were not at home and we discussed planning ahead next time, and not just going without letting anyone know that you are on your way.

There's an App for That

Life is a blank canvas, and you need to throw all the paint on it you can. —Danny Kaye

Life360. It's a GPS app and works like Sean's first cell phone—the Mi-Go phone when we needed GPS to track Sean's whereabouts by locating the address where the phone is. With all of his newfound independence riding the bus all over the county I needed to know where he was at all times.

Sean had strict instructions to leave his phone on at all times. He argued that he couldn't leave it on when he's in the movies. It's against the rules. And, of course, the movie rules trump Mom and Dad rules. Even though I showed him how to turn the sound off, he still refused to leave the phone on when he was in a movie theatre.

Sean transferred all of his iTunes to his iPhone 5, and I lost my most powerful discipline weapon. He learned to use Siri to convert his voice to send texts and to read his texts to him if there was a word he couldn't decode. He got his own Facebook page and would talk to post his posts. He constantly asked for new apps and new games, and the things he can do on that phone blow me away every day. We had to download the new bus route app "Mooove It." He downloaded a music video app and created custom special effects. I can't figure out how to do most of what he can do on that phone. If we had iPhones and iPads when Sean was younger, I know he would be reading better and have so much more knowledge than he does today.

Girlfriend's House

All journeys have secret destinations of which the traveler is unaware.
—Martin Buber

The same summer Sean decided he wanted to take the bus to his current girlfriend's house. She lived 40 minutes away by car in Newport Beach. He swore he knew the bus route and would say, "The 85 to the 89 to the 1 to the 57." He was speaking a foreign language to me. I accessed the OCTA bus Web site and it took me a few tries before I successfully figured out how to map out the route. The concern I had after figuring out the route was that he might get on the 1 South instead of the 1 North because they departed from the same location.

I planned ahead with his girlfriend's mother for a date and time when they would be home. She was on standby in case she needed to do any rescuing since I would be at work. Sean had to leave our house at 10 a.m., then he would have two bus changes before he arrived in Laguna Beach to do his third bus change to take the 1 North. Then he would change buses one more time in Newport Beach to the 57, would get off at the bus stop just outside his girlfriend's neighborhood, and walk the two blocks to her house.

Sean was instructed to call me at each bus change. When he called me at 11:50 to tell me he was on the 1 bus I knew he was on the southbound, instead of the northbound bus—the northbound bus didn't come until 12 noon.

"Mom, I'm on the 1 bus."

"Uh-oh, I think you got on the south not the north bus. The north bus doesn't come for another 10 minutes."

"No, it's the 1 bus."

"Is there anybody else on the bus?"

"Ya, lots of people."

"Ask someone if you are going to San Clemente or Newport Beach." I heard him ask another passenger, and indeed, he was heading the wrong way. The other passenger was kind enough to direct Sean when to get off to transfer to the 1 northbound. He actually got off the bus with Sean and pointed out the correct bus stop. Sean then had to cross busy Pacific Coast Highway.

Five buses and three and a half hours after he left our house he arrived at his girlfriend's house. Her mother called me and let me know he had made it there safely. A few minutes later, she texted me a photo of Sean . . . sound asleep on her couch.

Piano Man

Sing us a song, you're the piano man. — Piano Man, Billy Joel

Rick and I hosted Cool Club one weekend and investigated a Piano Bar that has dueling pianos and everybody sings along. We talked to the manager, and because they are also a restaurant, people under age 21 can enjoy the entertainment until the kitchen closes at 10 p.m. The music starts around 8:30 so we held Cool Club there. We went earlier and had dinner first. The group loved the music, especially Sean. He knew the words to every song. Rick couldn't believe how many songs Sean knew since many were from the '80s. It's because of *Glee*. *Glee* has many songs from the '80s so Sean knew them all.

Another couple hosted Cool Club there a few weeks later and one of the patrons actually asked the husband, "Why did you bring them here tonight?"

He thought she was going to say how cool that was and he replied, "They love it here." She was nasty. "They shouldn't be here." Then she went and found the manager and told him he should kick them out. The manager was beside himself with anger. He called the owners and asked if he could kick the woman out. They told him that if she did one inappropriate thing he could kick her out.

The manager then went to my friend and told him, "If she even looks at you guys wrong, rolls her eyes—anything—you tell me and she's out of here." After that, our group received celebrity treatment from the employees there because that nasty woman made such a big deal out of our inclusion.

For his nineteenth birthday we told Sean he wasn't having a birthday party. That he could go on a date with his girlfriend to the piano bar, but that was it. We planned a surprise party and had 16 of his friends waiting at the piano bar when he arrived. He loved his surprise party, and even got a little teary. That skipped a generation. Rick and I aren't real emotional people, but both of our mothers are, and so is Sean.

The two pianists who play and sing are very entertaining and very funny. Sean wanted to dance with his girlfriend to the song, "I Will Always Love You" by Whitney Houston. I helped him fill out the request card.

The pianist announced that Sean wanted a slow dance and asked everybody to sit down while he and his girlfriend danced. A few bars into the song Sean twirled her and the whole bar cheered them on. Sean was loving the spotlight so when the song was done, he kissed her—it sounded like the winning touchdown at the Super Bowl, everybody was cheering so loudly. Then Sean gestured for the microphone. The pianist gave it to him, and Sean took a knee and he proposed, *"Will you marry me?"* She nodded her head yes, and once again the crowd cheered loudly.

There was no ring, and Sean proposed all the time, but the crowd didn't know that. Sean received a lot of positive reinforcement, and every time he goes there the pianists know the routine. They are so funny when they see the Cool Club group. They warn the audience, "Tonight there will be a lot of Bieber Fever, and some Miley Cyrus Virus, but it will all end with Whitney Houston." And each time they allow Sean to take the microphone and propose to whoever his date is that night.

Transition: Year Two

All that is valuable in human society depends upon the opportunity for development accorded the individual. —Albert Einstein

During the IEP the prior spring I tried to gain some individualization for Sean's program. I volunteered to do some research over the summer and provide the district with a list of places that Sean would like to work. I felt they needed to get out of the box and truly individualize the program for each student. That didn't just include support at community college but also the work experiences. When I asked what their success rate was in placing students in paid work experiences when they graduated from the program they told me it was 2 percent. Two percent of the students who went through their transition program would become gainfully employed by the time they graduated. Disgusting. And nobody seemed concerned about improving that number.

I spent a few hours searching over the summer and created a list that included names, addresses, and phone numbers of every sport or entertainment-related place where Sean was interested in working. I made sure they were within the school district's geographic realm. I came up with 83 businesses. Golf courses, tennis clubs, recreation programs, Taco Bell locations, sports parks, Angel Stadium, and the Honda Center. Even schools with sports programs, bowling alleys, movie theatres, YMCA locations, and more. I e-mailed the list asking that they please develop a job for Sean at one place on the list.

The principal asked to meet with me, so we had yet another IEP meeting. The person in charge of the Career Start program attended and told me that they were going to develop jobs at their existing sites. They had no desire to think outside the box and no incentive to provide anything individualized to Sean. At this meeting we also modified Sean's IEP to show that he would not be attending the program on Mondays and Wednesdays since he would be in his community college classes. The classes he had chosen were Introduction to Modern Dance, Adapted Personal Fitness, and Adapted Stretch. He attended from 9 a.m. to 1:30 p.m.

The community college classes began 2 weeks before the transition program, and I took Sean to the campus to show him how to walk from the bus stop to his classes, then to the cafeteria and back to the classes. Thankfully, because they were all physical education classes, they were in the same building on campus, but that building is a good 15–20-minute walk from the bus stop. He had to walk up a hill, across the quad area of the campus, cross a bridge, go down some stairs, then cross a parking lot to get to his classes. It was quite the maze. I had attended the community college when I was younger but still needed a map to help me chart the path to Sean's classes from the bus stop. After locating the physical education building I showed him where the cafeteria was and how to walk back to his last class from there. We only did it that one time, and Sean was able to maneuver the path without any future reminders. His sense of direction has always been stellar.

When the fall semester of the transition program began, Sean was so disappointed. The teacher he was working so hard to impress over the summer had not selected him to be in her class. The whole summer he had stayed on his best behavior and complied with everything that teacher had told him to do, and he felt like he was a huge failure.

One good thing about staying in the first class was his friend Ben was now in that class. They had been friends for years, but because they attended different high schools they had never been in a class together before. Another good thing about Sean and Ben being in class was his mother Kristi and I were able to compare notes. Ben was going to receive speech therapy, and I had been told there was no speech therapy in the transition program. Sean started speech therapy again thanks to Kristi making sure I knew it was available.

By October, Ben had two different work experiences in place. He was working at a grocery store on one day and at a senior center on another day. He was working less than 2 hours at each one, but at least he was working. I waited another couple of weeks, and Sean still had not brought home a job packet.

I was sure Sean was being punished and not being placed in a job because I had him at community college 2 days a week and not at the transition program all 5 days. I e-mailed the teacher, and she told me that they were waiting to hear about the nursing home opportunity again. He was going to have the same job coach as the year before, and she was the one contacting the work site. I e-mailed her a few days later asking if she had heard from the nursing home. She responded, "I called him earlier today and he's supposed to call me back and give me a start date." This went on for 2 more weeks.

I finally e-mailed her again. "I've been in sales for over 20 years. When somebody says they will call you back with an answer, and then never calls you back, then the answer is 'no.' Please find Sean a job soon."

Sean was discouraged. On Tuesdays and Thursdays he was the only one in class with the teacher one-on-one. She was having him help her around the class, but he was bored stiff and started skipping school. He would leave our house as though he was going to school, but at the place where he changed buses, he would just go to McDonald's or a bagel shop and eat breakfast. I would get a call from the teacher that he wasn't at school, then I would activate his Life360 app and find him.

I couldn't *make* him do anything anymore. He would spend his day doing what he wanted to—his repertoire wasn't very diverse. He would eat breakfast, then go bowling. Or maybe catch a movie. And if he had enough money left over he would get a haircut. He had to spend every dollar in his pocket. He would end the day at the gym and take a shower. Sometimes he was home when I got home, but other times when I was finished working I would track him via Life360 and pick him up and bring him home.

When I limited his money he stole from me. I finally started keeping my purse in my bedroom, so he resorted to taking his coin jar in his backpack and spending his coins. He had at least 10 pounds of coins in his backpack. One day I picked him up at the gym, and he pulled out some bills to show me— he had $38 in cash. I was blown away. "Where did you get that money?"

"Burger King."

"What? Did you rob them?"

"No, my coins."

I went into Burger King to ask them what was up, and I didn't have to talk to anybody. There on the counter were stacks of quarters, nickels, dimes, and pennies. The manager had cashed Sean's coins out for him and lightened his backpack considerably. Nice guy.

Right before Thanksgiving I sent an e-mail to Sean's teacher and called an IEP. It was ridiculous that everybody in class had been working since the beginning of October and Sean was still in limbo.

When Sean returned after the Thanksgiving weekend he came home with a job packet. They had found him a job for 2 hours each day on Tuesdays and Thursdays at a Chili's restaurant. He had worked 4 hours each day 2 days a week at the food bank the previous year, but I was hoping the Chili's job hours would be extended after he got started.

Sean was so excited. He had done a volunteer stint at another restaurant with Special Olympics at a Tip-A-Cop fundraiser and worked with a waitress. He thought working in a restaurant was awesome.

When he came home from his first day at Chili's we asked him what he did. He lied to us. "I cleaned tables, I brought water to the tables, I cooked food in the microwave, I mopped the floor."

"Wow, they had you do a lot on your first day."

Thursday rolled around and at 9 a.m. his job coach called me.

"Sean's not at school yet, and we have to leave to go to Chili's." I was blown away. He had acted so excited about the job, but he still wasn't even at school? I checked Life360 and saw he was at McDonald's.

I called him, "What are you doing?"

"Eating breakfast."

"Why aren't you at school? They need to leave to go to Chili's, and you aren't there."

"I'm not doing that job again."

"What? I thought you liked it. What did you do on Tuesday?"

"They made me put a fork and a knife inside a napkin, and I don't like that."

I completely understood. Sean is a large muscle person. Fine motor skills are so difficult for him, and to have him roll silverware was a fine motor skill. I was so frustrated. Sean had been assessed for job interests and skills compatible with different types of jobs. I had provided them a list of 83 different places he would like to work, but still they couldn't get out of the box on the simpleton jobs. I said, "Sean, you can't do it this way. You have to call. You can quit, but you can't just not show up."

"OK, I quit."

"No, you don't tell *me* that you quit, you have to tell *them*."

The following Tuesday I drove Sean to school to make sure he actually made it there. His teacher, Sean, and I had an informal meeting in an empty classroom. His teacher said, "Sean, if you do a good job at Chili's then I can get you another job at Crunch Fitness."

My eyes bulged out of my head. *Seriously?* He had to work hard at something he didn't like—doing a task that that was physically very hard for him, before he could get a job someplace that he would *want* to work, doing work that he would be enjoy and experience success? I asked if I could speak privately with her. I was always careful to be respectful in front of Sean. He went back to class, and I said, "I gave a list of jobs to the principal and the Career Start person at Sean's IEP in August. Crunch Fitness was on that list, and I don't understand why he wasn't placed there in the first place. He isn't going back to Chili's.

In the real world, if you don't like a job, you quit. You don't have to do it better before you can do something you are better at, or something that you would prefer to do. He will continue to skip school if you force him to work some place he doesn't want to. He loved the food bank last year, and when he was in high school, he liked doing go-backs at the pharmacy, cleaning at the bagel shop, but he hated working at T. J. Maxx with the clothing. It's not that he doesn't want to work, he just needs something that is interesting and meaningful to him, where he can be social and physical."

One week later he began working at Crunch Fitness, cleaning the equipment. He did the job on four different occasions, then didn't want to do that one anymore either. After the Christmas break, I drove him to school once again, and we met with his teacher. She pulled out the notes from the job coach—a different job coach than he had the year before. There were pages of notes, he had worked a total of 8 hours, and this woman had documented everything.

- I told Sean to only put one pump of cleaning fluid on the cloth. He sprayed it twice so the cloth was too wet
- I told Sean to start cleaning another area of the gym and he ignored me
- Sean was watching TV and not working
- I sent Sean into the men's locker room to pick up towels. Twenty minutes later I had to send another student to get him
- Sean was in the men's locker room talking to himself and wouldn't come out

It went on and on and on. I'm not sure how much job coaching she could do when she was documenting every tiny detail of non-compliance. I also am not sure how Sean was supposed to be perfect at the job when he had only worked at it a whole 8 hours.

The transition program was next door to the school district's continuation high school where the students who had been expelled for drugs, weapons, or fighting attended school. Sean's teacher had an idea that he should learn how to clean gym equipment there—then perhaps he could return to Crunch Fitness.

The second semester of college was about to begin, and Rick and I decided to keep Sean at the transition program 5 days a week and have him take the community college Intermediate Bowling class in the afternoons after the transition program.

Sean cleaned gym equipment at the continuation school and did a good job, so they placed him back at Crunch Fitness. Crunch has many televisions, and Sean just couldn't stop being distracted by them. He told his teacher, "The TVs hurt my head," so back to the continuation school he went.

We called another IEP and with a lot of frustration Rick and I explained our concerns that Sean was wasting his time in the program and how damaging it was that he didn't have meaningful work. We explained that through his behavior he was trying to communicate that he was bored and was able to make a more interesting day for himself than they could provide. The principal had an idea, and she proposed it to Sean. "Sean, would you want to work here at my school?" (She was referring to our district's illegal segregated school site where students with disabilities are all educated away from the regular education population from ninth grade through age 22.) Sean jumped at the chance. He would continue cleaning gym equipment at the continuation school on Tuesdays, and his new job on Thursdays was being an aide in a PE class, helping the students, and then making lunch in the cafeteria for the students.. He liked this job, and he knew a few of the students who went to the school too.

I had another idea that I proposed. Since Sean wasn't making it all the way to the transition program each day, perhaps we should start over and have the little yellow bus pick him up in the mornings again, but he could take the public transportation bus back home in the afternoons. This was agreed upon, but because of the bureaucracy of the bus company it would still take 2 weeks to get the bus set up.

The following Tuesday he skipped school again, and then on Thursday as he was traveling to the segregated school he fell asleep on the public bus. He woke up one stop too late, and was confused and couldn't figure out how to backtrack to the place he should have disembarked. His job coach was waiting at his bus stop to walk with him to the school. When he didn't get off the bus she called him, but he didn't answer. He thought he was in trouble. As a consequence for skipping school on Tuesday we had told him he would be grounded on Friday, and unable to go with the class on CBI to see the movie, *The Great and Powerful Oz*. He had been perseverating about missing the movie all week.

The teacher called me. "Can you track Sean on Life360? He didn't get off the bus." I tracked him and told her he was one stop past where he should be, and I asked that his job coach just go pick him up. I explained to her that when he thought he was in trouble he wouldn't answer his phone. Instead the teacher directed the job coach to come back to her class.

I had recently had foot surgery and was home on my couch. I was instructed not to walk on my foot and had a knee walker, which was very unwieldy, and I had to keep my foot elevated most of the day.

I followed Sean on the tracking app and saw he had gotten back on the bus and was heading in the wrong direction. Then I saw him get off the bus at a mall that has a movie theatre in it. Coincidentally, the same movie theatre that the class was going to be attending the next day to watch *The Great and Powerful Oz*.

The teacher called me again. "Where is Sean now?"

"He's at the mall where you guys are going tomorrow. I would bet you he's going to stay and watch the movie, because he knows he is going to have to stay home tomorrow and will miss it."

She said, "You have to go get him."

I was on the couch with my foot over my head and said, "Well, I'm supposed to be elevating my foot, and I know where he is. He's fine there. I'll deal with him when he gets home."

She said, "If you don't go get him I have to call the police. He is supposed to be in our care, and he can't be in the community unsupervised."

I almost lost it. Two weeks earlier a young man with Down syndrome, Ethan Saylor, had just died at the hands of untrained policemen at a movie theatre. The tragedy occurred because Ethan wanted to see a movie twice, and the off duty policeman working security at the theatre handcuffed Ethan, laid him on the ground and he died of asphyxia. I was certain Sean would not understand why police would be confronting him as well and would possibly react the same as Ethan had, and the results could be deadly for Sean too.

I was so angry they would consider calling the police on Sean when they refused to drive one block to pick him up when he got confused earlier in the day. I implored them not to call, and against doctor's orders, I got into the car and I went to the mall and found Sean easily.

Sean was surprised to see me. "What are you doing here?"

"Looking for you. What happened this morning?"

"I fell asleep. When I woke up I didn't know where I was."

"Why didn't you answer your phone?"

"I was scared. I was in trouble again."

"So what are you going to do?"

"Watch the movie."

"Will you come home with me?"

"No." He got up and started to run away from me.

I decided to just leave. I couldn't catch him if I wanted to, and what would I do with him if I did catch him? I called and e-mailed his teacher and told her that I had Sean with me. "Count Sean as absent. He is in my care, and I am responsible for him. If you were to send the police I am afraid he would run and things would escalate. I expect sending him on the little bus next week will alleviate the issue of him not making it to school because he won't have the freedom to skip and make inappropriate choices."

I then contacted Sean's Regional Center worker. I had tried repeatedly to transfer him into another program. I had tried to transfer him into one of the neighboring districts that actually individualized their transition programs. I had tried to transfer him into a day program, but was told that because of budget cuts the state wasn't funding day programs until age 22. The Regional Center worker called me back and was furious they had threatened to call the police on Sean. She was shocked. "Seriously? They wanted to call the police because he didn't go to school or work? When I don't come to work nobody sends the police after me. As an adult you have that choice. If you exercise that choice too much, you can get fired, but you have the choice."

If the teacher had sent his job coach one block away to pick him up as I had asked earlier that morning he would have been at work.

He enjoyed the movie, then came home.

Off the Grid

Living off the grid and being kind of an outlaw brings a dangerous reality.—Ron Perlman

When Sean doesn't want to be found he will turn his phone off. We call this "Going off the grid." Sometimes he does it to avoid something he doesn't want to do. Other times it is when he has too much money and is determined to spend it all and he doesn't want anybody to stand in his way. Sometimes it's both.

Sean was 19 and I had carefully scheduled an orthodontist appointment during the Christmas break so Sean wouldn't miss school and I wouldn't miss much work. I made the mistake of telling him that I would be back from work at noon to take him to lunch, then we would go to the orthodontist appointment. When I got home he was nowhere to be found, and his phone was off so I couldn't track him. I didn't think he had any money, and I knew he didn't have a current bus pass, so I checked my purse to see if he had taken his ATM card, and sure enough, he had lifted it out of my purse again. I went onto the bank Web site to see if he had used it and found the paper trail. He had first gone to the grocery store and purchased a 1-month bus pass. Then he went to Carl's Jr. and had breakfast. His next purchase was at the movie theatre around 10:30 a.m. I jumped in the car and went to the theatre. I looked at the movie titles and assumed he was at the 3-hour-long *Hobbit* movie. I talked to the manager of the theatre, and he let me enter to find Sean. The theatre was packed and

I couldn't pick Sean out of the crowd, so I waited outside until the movie ended at 1:00. Sean didn't leave the theatre. I had picked the wrong movie. Later, he told me he saw a different movie I would have never thought he would choose—turns out he had left the theatre before I had even arrived.

I called Rick and had him go online and check the bank again, and his next purchase was at the bowling alley. By then, I didn't have time to get him and make it to the orthodontist on time. So I called and cancelled the appointment. I went back to work and Rick went to the bowling alley to pick Sean up. He said Sean was amazed when he saw Rick.

"How did you find me?"

Rick didn't tell him we tracked him through his ATM purchases. We have to keep one trick in our bag.

IEP Meeting Year Three Planning

My mother said I must always be intolerant of ignorance but under-standing of illiteracy. That some people, unable to go to school, were more educated and more intelligent than college professors. — Maya Angelou

As we met to plan year 3 of the transition Sean didn't bother to create a PowerPoint. Nobody had listened to the first two he created. I had done some research on how the other two districts were supporting students in community college classes and found out that both had classes *on* their community college's campus. Then they had a re-quirement that three to five students needed to select the same class, and they would send an aide with them. As a part of their program they helped with homework as well. The principal of Sean's program was certain they were only taking the "special education" classes of-fered at the community college, but the person I talked to assured me they assisted the students in any classes they selected. She gave me a quick list off the top of her head:

Reading Skills Lab
Beginning Golf
Reading and Voc LAB—ESL
Life Management
Sanitation and Safety
Power Yoga

Memory Skills
Phonetics—Read/Spell
Intro to Jazz Dancing
Basic Computer Skills
Pilates Conditioning
Stretch/Flex/Conditioning
Cardio Kickboxing
Language Development PRAC(S)
Contemp. Health Issues
Cardiovascular Cond(S)
Keyboarding
Weight Training
Various Drama and Theatre Arts Classes
Health
Careers
Various Art Classes
Cooking (one student even received his Culinary Arts Certificate)

As my experiences in primary and secondary school had been, I believed it was necessary to have a district administrator present when you are asking for something that is continually denied. The district Special Education director refused to attend Sean's IEP.

Sean wasn't interested in taking academic classes, but he had made an F in both his acting and dance classes. I knew why in the acting class, but I didn't know why in the dance class. It is possible that he didn't attend the class, but he came home with some video on his phone of the girls dancing, so he had been there some of the time. He wanted to take a real cooking class, but would need support for that as well. He was going to need to retake the acting and dance classes to clear his F grades, and I didn't want to enroll him without support.

We pressed them once again for support at the community college during Sean's IEP, preparing for his third wasted year of transition. Sean provided them with a letter asking that they deny his support at community college in written form, and they provided us with this letter:

Dear Sean McElwee,

On April 23, 2013, during your Annual IEP meeting, you submitted a letter requesting support from the transition program so (you) can participate in career-related courses at Community College. You further clarified during the IEP meeting that the support you are requesting is in the form of an aide to assist you in a course of your choice.

District staff have considered your request. In accordance with the provisions of Education Code Part 30, California Code of Regulations—Title 5, Chapter 4.5, this shall serve as notice of proposed/refused actions by the District with regard to your education.

The District has declined to fund aide support at community college because:

Our transition team provides supports and experiences to aid in achieving your postsecondary goals. These are goals pertaining to your education/training, employment and independent living upon exiting special education services. As indicated on page one of your Individualized Transition Plan, upon completion of school you plan to take career-related courses allowing you to progress in your desired field of theatre arts.

The District offers the following support to you toward your attainment of your identified postsecondary goal on your ITP in the area of education:
- Provide experience using Orange County Transit to advance your mobility options throughout the community;

- Provide experience navigating a college campus, reading a catalogue, and exploring the community college Web site;
- Provide a variety of vocational experiences to strengthen your skills and explore areas of interest;
- Provide accommodations to your school schedule should you decide to take a course at the community college;
- Provide whole group community college experiences taking a course in physical fitness; and
- Provide instruction and training to build your vocational, communication, and social skills to increase your likelihood of success toward your postsecondary goals.

The District has offered the following Free and Appropriate Public Education (FAPE) for you:

- Specialized Academic Instruction SDC 5 x 360 minutes daily Group
- Speech/Language Therapy 1 x 15 minutes weekly Collaboration

The above referenced FAPE offer has been recommended by the IEP team based on your goals and objectives and has been reasonably calculated to provide you with educational benefits tailored to meet your unique needs. To determine your unique needs, the District has performed the following assessments:

Career Decision-Making System Revised 7/3/12
Oral and Written Language Scales Second Edition 11/6/12
Goldman-Fristoe 2 Test of Articulation 11/6/12
Street Skills Survival Questionnaire 4/23/13
Authentic Assessment 4/23/13
Observations 4/23/13, 11/6/12, 7/312

The District continues to offer you a FAPE consisting of the appropriate placement and services in the least restrictive environment as outlined above. The placement and services are based upon all assessments conducted by the team and additional information provided, including your input.

Finally, please be advised that an individual with a disability has protection under the procedural safeguards of the Individuals with Disabilities Education Act (IDEA). In that regard, enclosed, please find a copy of your procedural safeguards. The sources which you may contact to obtain assistance in understanding the provisions of the procedural safeguards are as follows:

Office of Administrative Hearings
Attention: Special Education Division
2349 Gateway Oaks Drive suite 200
Sacramento, CA 95833-4231

California Department of Education
P.O. Box 944272
Sacramento, CA 94244-2720

Should you have any questions, please feel free to contact me.

Sincerely,

Principal

From the letter above, "Our transition team provides support and experiences to aid in achieving your postsecondary goals. These are goals pertaining to your education/training, employment and independent living upon exiting special education services. As indicated on page one of your Individualized Transition Plan, upon completion of school you plan to take career-related courses allowing you to progress in your desired field of theatre arts."

Did they see "theatre arts" was listed as his desired field on his transition plan? Then they included it in his denial but have no services provided for him to achieve his desired field.

I sent the letter to our Regional Center to show that the transition program could not provide Sean with his individualized needs, and they also refused to help and again was told that he would not qualify for them to fund services until he was 22 years old. I also contacted an attorney to see about filing a Fair Hearing. I was advised that the law didn't clarify transition services clearly enough, and that several other people were losing their Fair Hearings, so we didn't pursue a Fair Hearing with the school district.

Sean attended the summer program again, had a lot of fun at concerts, the county fair, beach days, movies, and amusement parks. So much for a meaningful education.

Moving Out

I give you this to take with you: Nothing remains as it was. If you know this, you can begin again, with pure joy in the uprooting. —Judith Minty

Sean was 12 years old when some of the challenger sports coaches told us there was a nonprofit agency being formed to provide an Independent Supported Living facility for our kids when they became adults. We stayed in the loop as they researched various housing options. When Sean was 15 they purchased a property that had started as a motel, and later was transformed into assisted living apartments for senior citizens.

It was a dump and needed a lot of work before it could be inhabited. While the price was amazing for a property that could house 50 adults in their own apartments two blocks from the beach, it needed around a million dollars of work before anybody could inhabit the property. Included on the property was a common dining room and a very large activity room. Because of city fire codes, the residents wouldn't be allowed to have microwaves or other cooking abilities in their room, but a small college dorm refrigerator would be allowed.

I joined the fundraising committee and organized the first fundraiser along with a plea to the television show *Extreme Makeover Home Edition*. That was going to be the most expeditious and cost-effective way to get adults moved in . . . but if the show did select us it would be ready much too soon for Sean to be able to move in. The minimum age would be 18 years old—he needed the project to take at least 3 years so he could be one of the first residents.

We invited all of our sports friends to the combination fundraiser and plea for *Extreme Makeover* and ended up with around 75 teens and adults with a variety of disabilities and their parents and siblings to be filmed for our application video. We had group camera shots in a few different locations on the property, complete with signs for the potential future residents to hold while they shouted, "Please Help us, Extreme Makeover." And, "We Love You, Ty." Sean had a blast at the event, and even participated in the individual interviews that were taped to edit together for the 30-minute plea video. Being involved in this project got Sean involved and thinking about moving out, and we geared our conversations toward that goal as well. When he wanted to do something and we said no, we would add, "But when you move out you can do that." He craved a taste of freedom away from his pesky parents.

Sean's friend Chris was there for the plea to *Extreme Makeover*, but as he looked at the beautiful Pacific Ocean view, he told his mother, "I'm not living here."

She asked, "Why not?"

"Tsunamis."

We all got a chuckle out of that . . . until the tsunami hit Japan a year later, and Chris ran around saying, "See? I told you so."

Unfortunately *Extreme Makeover Home Edition* was in its final season and all of the projects had been selected. Ours was not on the list. Having an empty building to fund raise for was excruciating. We all knew that it would be easier once people were living there, but every dime had been tapped out of the parents of potential future residents and now it was time to go to the community at large. After 2 years, enough funds were raised to hire a director and assistant director. They began preparations to interview prospective residents.

Since Sean had been involved in the process of preparing the property for inhabitation for what was ultimately 4 years, he had been looking forward to the day he could move into his own apartment on the property. He knew some of the other residents who planned to move in and he had all kinds of ideas how to decorate his place. We had never let him have a television in his bedroom at our home. For Christmas, we purchased a television for him and told him he could take it to his new apartment with him. He told people he was moving there even before he was accepted. We were cracking down behaviorally at home and not allowing him permission do everything he wanted to. He was acting like a typical teenager going through the separation phase of development. Rebellion was a daily reminder that Sean didn't want to live with us anymore. By being strict we were also compelling his desire to gain independence.

Rick's company contracted to do the security system, including video surveillance cameras in the common areas, key-coded gated entries, and sensors on each room's door in order to monitor any potential late-night exits from the rooms.

During the third year of Sean's transition program (he was 19 years old), we received the call to come and interview for one of the 50 spots. Sean answered all of the interview questions to their satisfaction. When they asked why he wanted to move in he responded with thick disdain in his voice, "To get away from my parents." He received his acceptance letter at the end of March with an expected move-in to be in July.

Sean was so excited. He told everyone he was moving. We measured his apartment, and I created a floorplan on graph paper and calculated the size of furniture that would fit in the room. We started boxing up the items he wanted to take from home and made an area in the garage for them. We shopped for a combination TV stand/shelf unit and a free-standing mirrored wardrobe since the closet in his room was pretty small. Sean has a wardrobe collection to be rivaled by most girls.

Sadly, his current girlfriend's parents made them break up. Sean was going to have his own bachelor pad, and they were afraid of his independence. We later found out that boys and girls wouldn't be allowed in each other's apartments unsupervised, so those fears were unfounded. But we honored her family's wishes and facilitated the breakup. Sean was heartbroken. I don't think her family ever told her why they broke up, but I had to tell Sean why.

Each weekend Sean and I went and walked around the town of his future home. It's a great small beach town, with a lot of restaurants. We explored so he would know where everything was located. We ate at many different restaurants, and Sean would tell everyone, "I'm moving here."

At one of the beaches are sand volleyball courts, and two half-court basketball courts. I imagined Sean hanging out at the beach all day, boogie boarding, building sand castles, and playing volleyball and basketball. This was going to be a perfect place for him to live and truly be included in the community.

Sean has had a lot of opportunities to meet and be photographed with famous people at Best Buddies and Special Olympics events. I made posters with his celebrity photos and framed them for décor. We shopped for bedding, and he selected a zebra print comforter and accessories. Everything was ready to go, then, as many construction projects go, the move-in date was delayed.

The longer it took, the more Sean was becoming anxious about the move. Maybe I had made too big a deal of it. I had him doing one thing every day to prepare for the move. We selected which shirts he would take on one day. Another, we selected which shorts, and decided he needed a few more pairs of shorts and went shopping on another day. I kept the move at the forefront of his consciousness.

Then one day he flipped out. We were going to use a label-maker to put his name on his Wii games, and he told me he didn't want to take them. He is obsessed with his Wii games, but he only wanted to take one of his 20-plus games. We asked him why and found out he had some fears about the move.

Sean was afraid that the other residents and strangers could steal his things. Being an only child I knew a roommate situation would have never worked with him, so he was going to have a private room and bathroom. Nobody ever had to go into his room if he didn't want them to, but he was insistent that they would break in and take whatever they wanted. I think he had seen too many movies.

"The bad guys are going to run in and just take my stuff."

"What bad guys? Bad guys won't be there."

"They will, and they will take my games and my money and my movies."

Rick was able to take him to the property and show him the cameras, the locks on the gates, and point out that his door would have its own lock and key. Sean's whole body relaxed and, finally relieved, he said, "Oh good." He still wasn't completely convinced that Dad knew what he was talking about, but he wasn't so fixated on those fears any longer.

Living Options

Freedom is realizing you have a choice. —T. F. Hodge

We had attended several seminars on living options. Sean and I had participated in living option tours several times through our Regional Center (Department of Developmental Disabilities). The options we had seen were:

Family Homes—Where a family takes an adult with a disability into their home to live as part of their family. We know two adults with Down syndrome living with young couples, and this has been a great option for them.

Group Homes—An agency operates a home for adults with disabilities. There may be full-time staff onsite, or may not be, depending on the needs of the adults who live there. We know a couple of adults with different disabilities living in group homes. Some have to share a room, others have private rooms. Sean was raised as an only child, and we didn't think he would do well sharing anything in a group home.

Supported Living—Live in your own apartment or house that is leased. Live alone or with a roommate. Support is provided based on the individual needs. We know one adult who has someone come for only 3 hours a week to make sure his bills are paid, his home is cleaned, and his grocery shopping is done. We know another who has two supporting adults 24/7 with him at all times because of behavior issues. This option is individualized for the person's needs. His parents refer to them as "his staff" since there are eight different people who take 8-hour shifts around the clock, including days off.

Independent Living—Few supports necessary, or supports that are naturally provided by friends and family and not paid staff members.

Rick and I felt like the Supported Living Apartments would provide the supervision of supported living, with the feel of independent living. With adults living in individual apartments (some have roommates) but with the support staff onsite, there is a greater level of supervision, mixed with the privacy of your own apartment. Another difference we thought it would provide a sense of community with 50 adults living there and many friendships previously existing and more being formed.

We met one young man who had lived in his own apartment with some supported living staff who came in the evenings to help him make dinner. He was thrilled when he heard about these apartments. He was so lonely. His neighbors didn't talk to him. He was excited to have neighbors that he could walk next door and watch TV with, or invite to go to a movie or elsewhere. All of his friends still lived at home with their parents and weren't able to ride the bus independently so he had nobody to hang out with. We felt like this would provide Sean the social stimulation he loves and needs, along with the ability to go into his room and have some quiet time alone.

I Don't Have to—You Can't Make Me

Defiance is beautiful. The defiance of power, especially great or over-whelming power, exalts and glorifies the rebel—Edward Abbey

Sean was tasting freedom. He was a few months away from moving out, and he was defying us in every way. I couldn't get him to do any chores around the house, and he was acting so entitled. It was frustrating and embarrassing as well. Rick concocted a great idea. We were 3 weeks away from Christmas and feeling like Sean didn't deserve anything from Santa—who he still believed in. Rick added a phone number to Sean's phone when he wasn't looking. It was our neighbor's cell number, but the name Rick programmed into the phone said, "Santa Claus."

We were eating dinner and talking about things that Sean needed to do . . . laundry, pick up his room, do the dishes, and he was handily telling us that he wasn't going to do any of those things when his phone rang. His eyes were huge when he read who was calling.

"Santa?"

"Hello? Yes, this is me, Santa."

He looked at us and mouthed, "It's Santa!"

We said, "Put it on speaker."

And there was our neighbor's voice, "Ho! Ho! Ho! Sean, I can see everything you are doing. I see you when you're sleeping. I know when you're awake. I know when you've been bad or good. Are you listening to your parents? They need your help around the house."

Sean put his hand over his mouth and to himself said, "Oh my gosh." Then to Santa, "Oh, Santa, I'll be better. I'm going to do the dishes tonight, and then I'll do my laundry tomorrow. I promise I'll be good."

Rick was very proud of himself, and Sean snapped out of his entitled mood and started helping around the house again. We did have to erase the number so he didn't try to call Santa back the next day—and the disappearance of the number in his contacts made the whole experience even more magical.

Ex-Girlfriend

Algebra is my favorite subject . . . because you can replace my X without asking me Y.—Unknown

We found out that one of Sean's ex-girlfriends was going to move into the apartments also. Tori and Sean had broken up about a year earlier, and it wasn't pretty. Sean had taken her to a dance, then ditched her to hang out with Ben. As I drove them home from the dance she chastised Sean the whole way, "You left me alone, and I didn't know anybody there. That was so mean." The next day I told him that he needed to call and apologize to her. He refused to apologize. A week later she texted him, "We aren't working out, I want to break up."

I was saying good night to him that night, and he said, "Don't look at my phone."

"Oh, okay."

The minute he was asleep I looked at his phone, expecting to find YouTube videos of scantily clad female WWE wrestlers—like I had the last time he told me not to look at his phone—but instead, I saw Tori's text, and his video reply, "Tori, you a bitch."

Nice. The next minute I was e-mailing her parents an apology. Both Sean and Tori thought the other one had dumped them and every event we had been to after the breakup Sean had asked if Tori would be there. He was very nervous about seeing her again.

I knew if they just appeared living in the same complex that the drama would ensue so we invited her parents and her over to dinner and encouraged her and Sean to become friends. They seemed to be all right. I was worried that if he became extremely frustrated and anxious he might revert to hitting like he had in intermediate school—the most anxious time in his life. So I sought out a behaviorist/social skills coach for him. I had her in place before move in, and she was a great counselor for Sean. She was teaching him phrases and ways to escape stressful situations when they arose. One technique was to tell the person that he didn't want to talk to that he had to go to the bathroom, then walk to his room, and when he returned, not sit next to that person.

There were some events at the property that were held in preparation for move in that we made sure Sean attended. One Saturday, a nonprofit group came and organized a planting on the property. They planted grapes, avocado trees, and fruit trees around the property. They planted vegetables in the planters to be harvested and eaten by the residents. At this event Sean and Tori were civil to each other.

Another time there was a housewarming party where each future resident got to open a donated wrapped gift of items that would be used in the kitchen or elsewhere on the property. Sean and Tori were polite, but basically ignored each other. I thought everything was going to be all right on that front, but kept the behaviorist in place just in case.

Final Details

As long as you're moving, it's easier to steer. —Anonymous

One of my best friend's daughters took a summer internship at the apartments to help the directors complete the many final details necessary in order for 50 adults to begin their transition to living there.

Two weeks before move in the director sent an SOS e-mail requesting help for the next day. As a part of the state licensing agreement they had to provide beds for the residents and had just found out the company that was donating the beds wasn't going to deliver them to the rooms, but just drop them on the driveway. I asked Sean if he would like to move beds into the rooms, or go on one of his outings during the summer transition program. He chose to help, so my friend's daughter picked him up, and he used his muscles to move beds. I felt like the more he could volunteer for things onsite that he would feel more of a sense of ownership. A week later he also helped move dressers and nightstands in.

Both times he took the bus back home after moving the items in and easily knew the correct stops to change buses and successfully made it home.

Move in Day

Mama, if that's movin' up then I'm movin' out. — Billy Joel, "Movin' Out (Anthony's Song)"

After a few construction delays the license was granted on a hot August Wednesday. Sean was on summer break from his transition program that didn't start back up until the Thursday after Labor Day. We received an e-mail that Sean could move in 3 days later on Saturday. We were definitely ready. Sean volunteered in the children's ministry at church with a man named Todd who had offered to assemble the IKEA furniture for us. We called him, and thankfully, he was available at the last minute. On Friday, several of our friends came and loaded their cars and SUVs with Sean's possessions and we were ready for move in day.

While we put the room together Sean was running around with some of the staff using his muscles to help move things for other residents. It was around 5:00 when I hung the last picture on the wall. He was ready for us to leave and kept telling us, "Good-bye. Good-bye already." So we left, exhausted and excited for him to spend the first night in his new home.

I Coped

It is what it is. Isn't that how these things always go? They are what they are. We just get to cope. —Mira Grant

I had micromanaged every moment of Sean's life. I planned his activities so he never sat still for a moment. I drove or arranged for his transportation to each activity. Coming up to the move in date he had some activity planned almost every day, and I had been the one who coordinated each of them. And when he moved out it just stopped . . . no tapering off. It just stopped. I didn't know what to do with myself.

Most parents see their teens get a driver's license, then they independently plan their own activities and aren't home so much, then they leave for college. They get a gradual tapering off of parental input and participation. I didn't have that. I was cut off. Cold turkey. As I wandered through the house I wasn't sure what to do next.

The day after move in was Sunday, and we did pick Sean up to volunteer at church. Afterward, we took him back to his apartment, then Rick and I walked around town and went out to dinner.

On Monday, Rick had to stop me. I wanted to go see Sean. I *did* go on Tuesday during lunch. As I entered the dining room Sean was sitting with some new friends and looked at me and said, "What are you doing here?"

Okay, I was okay, he was okay. I left feeling better. And then the staff filled me in . . . Drama, tremendous drama. Tori and Sean were not coexisting peacefully.

He had told some boys they were going to get back together—and they had told her—and she was mad. She thought he was limiting her options with the other boys by telling people they were getting back together. They were both going to the staff and tattling on each other. She was playing head games with him. They had some yelling matches.

The staff began to call it, "As the Independence Turns." The soap opera was playing itself out. I realized after the first week that I had moved my son into 24/7-junior-high-land. And then Gail moved in.

One week after move in Rick and I went to take several residents to a local art festival. This city has a free trolley that runs all summer, and it makes it very easy to transport a group of people around town. We asked the staff to see which residents were interested in going, and they had about seven people rounded up when we arrived. We were looking forward to getting to know them and knew that the best way to help Sean build relationships is to participate in activities away from home together. We looked forward to helping Sean to make some connections and to give him a break from the drama that was happening at the apartments.

When we arrived Sean was helping with chores, emptying trash into the big bin . . . but he wasn't using both hands to carry the trash bag. His left hand was holding the hand of a very cute girl with Down syndrome who we had not met before. Gail had moved in the night before and was a new resident. Sean asked if she could go with us to the art festival, and of course, we said, "Yes."

Now, there are two types of girls with Down syndrome. There's the, "Love the one you're with," and the "Loyal to the bitter end." We all hopped onto the trolley and rode down to the art festival. Sean and Gail sat next to each other. He put his arm around her, and she snuggled in. We had hoped to help him make some guy friends, but he had no interest in anybody but Gail.

Our new friends and Sean enjoyed looking at art. They made a necklace at a craft booth and a print at the printmaking booth. Then we all sat down and ate lunch and waited for the fashion show to begin.

As the fashion show was about to begin Sean sat next to Gail and she sat next to another resident, Kevin. Gail and Kevin started talking, and Sean was watching the fashion show. All of a sudden Sean jumped up and looked at Gail and Kevin with a panicked expression. She didn't seem to notice. Sean didn't say anything to them, but he then looked at me and said, "I'm outta here." And he took off. I chased after him to ask what happened, but he raced out of the festival and jumped on the next trolley before I could catch up to him. I went back to our table and Rick and I were a little disappointed. We had wanted to spend the day with Sean, we had brought the other residents so he could build a relationship with them, but we didn't want to be there without him.

When the fashion show ended we gathered everybody and headed back to the apartments on the trolley. We later found out what had happened.

When Gail and Kevin were talking she was actually flirting with him. He has autism and didn't pick up on her social cues, so she said to him, "I like you—like a boyfriend." That was what Sean had heard and that had upset him enough to make him bolt from the festival. The staff told me what happened next.

As Sean went to dinner that evening Gail was waiting outside the dining room for him. Turns out Kevin had told her that he just wanted to be friends and didn't want a girlfriend. Now, she was trying to repair the damage she had done. "Sean, I like you better than Kevin—I want to get back together."

Sean would have none of that. "No, Gail. You cheated on me. We're through."

As this conversation was taking place Tori walked up and realized she has some competition and she chimes in, "Sean, I love you. I want to get back together after all. Will you be my boyfriend again?"

That's what Sean had wanted all along, "YES. Yes, Tori, I want to get back together. Gail, we're through."

The ensuing drama was tremendous. I could have never imagined the next 2 weeks. Reality is much more interesting than anything I could have dreamed up . . . and if there had been a reality television show there, well, they could have paid the mortgage off by now.

Between Sean's SSI and additional money that we pitched in for rent we allowed him a budget of $100 a month for spending money. Since all three of his meals were provided, along with three snacks each day he didn't need a lot of money for anything. They even packed lunches for people going to work and school. Tori and Sean spent his entire $100 budget in the next 4 days as they went out to dinner at a different restaurant every evening.

Tori and Sean were quite the item and all the buzz with the residents. I stopped in one day and another resident, Carey, stopped me to talk about them. "Sean and Tori sure are enjoying themselves. I used to have a girlfriend, but she broke up with me. She didn't like farm animals."

I was dying, holding in the laughter as he continued. "I talk about farm animals all the time and she didn't like that."

The staff asked me to talk to Sean about kissing in private. Turns out he and Tori were in the game room, and they started laughing loudly to get everybody to look at them, then they kissed a long, passionate kiss. Their romance was stirring up the other residents.

Sharing Is Caring

Love only grows by sharing. You can only have more for yourself by giving it away to others. —*Brian Tracy*

Dave was another resident who was around 35 years old. He had Down syndrome and had previously lived in a group home before moving to the apartments. He had gone on our outing to the art festival and told us he was just on vacation and that he wasn't moving there permanently. He was very charming. While watching Sean and Tori he fell in love with the idea of love. Dave made the decision that he was going to get himself a girlfriend too, because Sean and Tori looked like they were having so much fun.

It was the fourth day of Sean and Tori's resumed romance. Sean and Tori were at a restaurant. I was told that Dave went around the dining room to the 18 girls who were present and asked each one of them, "Will you be my girlfriend?" I can imagine how special the girls felt as he worked his way around the room when he was told "no," then moving to the next girl with the same question. All 18 said "no." So Dave hatched an idea. It was obvious to him that the only girl living in the apartments that *wanted* a boyfriend was Tori. So he decided that Sean would just have to share.

Dave knocked on Sean's door. "Sean, it's my turn to date Tori now."

Sean slammed the door in his face and called me. He could barely speak he was crying so hard. "Mom. Tori's going out with Dave now." The tears were flowing.

I couldn't imagine Tori liking Dave. He was much different than Sean was. I was sure there was a misunderstanding. I tried to calm Sean down, but before I could give him my motherly advice he hung up on me.

He stormed up to Tori's room and knocked on her door, and when she answered he started yelling at her, "We're through. You cheated on me with Dave."

Tori had no idea what Sean was talking about. But she knew she didn't want a boyfriend who was going to yell at her, so she broke up with him.

Sean's transition program didn't start for another week and a half. He stayed in his room, depressed and sad, and only came out to eat. He watched his romance movies and past seasons of *Glee* over and over again. The staff told me he was coming to the dining room, but he was eating alone. I was devastated. He had lived there less than 2 weeks. Rick and I went that weekend and took him out to dinner. We talked about relationships and how messy they can be. His social skills coach helped him understand what had happened and how he could ask some clarifying questions if there was ever a next time, instead of yelling.

I asked him, "Do you want to move back home?"

He looked at me like I had asked him to stick needles in his eyes. "No way."

So even as he rode the emotional roller coaster of independence, unrequited love, and cheating women, he wanted nothing to do with living with his parents again.

Sean's social skills coach came to his apartment a few times to meet with him onsite. One day as their session was wrapping up another resident asked Sean who she was. He responded, "She's helping me to be a better person." He was comfortable talking to her, and she was doing him a lot more good than my motherly advice.

Two New Rules

If you come to a fork in the road, take it. —Yogi Berra

The staff at the apartments realized that dating was throwing a whole new spin on the first couple of weeks of living there. So they decided, thanks to Sean, to institute two new rules:

1. You must live there for 1 month before you can date another resident.
2. If you break up with a boyfriend or girlfriend, you must wait 2 weeks before you can date someone else.

When the residents pointed out that Sean and Tori had dated before living there 1 month, the staff rationalized that they had known each other before moving there, so that's why they were allowed to date before the 1-month rule. They explained that you have to know someone as a friend first before you can know if you have enough in common in order to date them. They were doing a good job of teaching about relationships. I was glad I had hired some help to reinforce that message and give Sean some tools he could use.

We would frequently park at the apartment, then walk with Sean to the grocery store to refill his little refrigerator with drinks and snacks or go out to eat at a local restaurant. One day soon after the Tori breakup we walked past an upscale Italian restaurant. Sean started walking faster and said, "Don't go in there."

"Why not?"

"Just don't."

We assumed that may have been one of the restaurants that he and Tori went to, and they might not have had enough money to pay the tab. I didn't go in there. I didn't want to know.

Another time we were there to take Sean out, and one resident had borrowed somebody's swim trunks and was heading off to the beach with a friend. Unfortunately, the trunks were about three sizes too small and a staff member was trying to reason with him, to see if he could borrow some larger trunks from someone else. Finally exasperated, she said, "Now what would your mother think of you going to the beach in trunks that were too small?"

He didn't skip a beat. "Well, my mother's not here now, is she?"

Rick and I frequently had to quickly move into a side room or just leave so we wouldn't be caught laughing so hard.

New Girlfriend

When in a relationship, a real man doesn't make his woman jealous of others, he makes others jealous of his woman. —Steve Maraboli

Sean waited the requisite 2 weeks before he declared his intentions to date Macy. Macy was adorable, used a wheelchair, and Sean was smitten. Turns out he had had his eye on her since the planting had happened. At the planting he had told her sister that he was going to date her . . . so he did. The apartments are on a very steep street, and Macy had a manual wheelchair so she had to be driven in a car to get in and out of there. Sean learned how to remove the large wheels and fold her chair so it fit into our car's trunk. She came to church with us, out to dinner, and to Sean's Young Life High Rollers' Club. He invited her to Cool Club, and they bowled on a Special Olympics Bowling Team together. I thought all was well, then she posted on Facebook, "In a complicated relationship with Sean McElwee."

I asked her mother what was going on. She told me that they kept breaking up and getting back together. But Sean said they weren't breaking up. Just like when anybody dates, there are "misunderstandings."

Sean was having a fantasy of moving to New York, and he kept talking about moving there. It turns out that Macy's interpretation was that he wanted to break up with her.

Sean came home over Thanksgiving weekend, leaving his apartment to collect dust for a few days. But he and Macy conspired a way to see each other and planned a movie date. Her mother brought her to the theatre, and Sean and I met them there. It was reminiscent of the times before he moved out when I drove on the dates and found myself with a couple of free hours, time to read my current book. They selected the movie *Frozen* and entered the theatre with many families, including their children who were under the age of 10.

After the movie I asked them how they liked it. Sean said, "There was a lot of kissing."

Clarifying, I asked, "There was a lot of kissing in the movie?"

"No, Macy and I kissed a lot."

Always emphasizing the privacy, I responded, "There were a lot of kids at that movie. I hope you didn't freak any parents out."

Sean paused for a moment, thinking, then said, "No, they couldn't see. The chairs are tall, and we were down low."

Apparently Macy had transferred out of her wheelchair into a movie theatre chair, and I had been in that theatre before. The seats did have high backs.

There was some miscommunication between them, as there frequently was when Sean dated. Between different receptive language skills and different expressive language skills misunderstandings were extremely common. Four months after move in they were still dating, and we transferred the social skills coach from helping Sean avoid confrontations into helping them build relationship skills and work on communication. I had wanted to do this with Sean's previous girlfriends, and it was great to have another parent who understood the challenges of dating with an intellectual disability. Whether they stayed together or not, the communication skills they learned would transfer into other relationships.

Transition: Year Three

First they ignore you, then they laugh at you, then they fight you, then you win. — *Mahatma Gandhi*

Sean's transition program started 2 weeks after he had moved into his supported independent living apartment. The city was in a different school district, but that district coincidentally shared the transition program with the school district he had been raised in, so unfortunately, that would remain the same. They sent an aide to bus train Sean and two other residents who were also attending the transition program. They had to catch the public bus at 6:30 a.m. to arrive for the 8:30 start time. Sean knew the way and had no problem maneuvering the bus changes to and from his apartment.

Sean had finally moved up to the class he wanted to be in, but was once again disappointed because his friend Ben was still in the other class. He was learning that you can't have it all. One evening we were eating dinner at a restaurant near his new home, and Sean asked the owner if he could have a job as a bus boy. I explained that Sean had a job coach through his transition program and that he could have support onsite that would teach Sean the job duties and he wouldn't have to pay Sean while he was learning the job. After he learned the job it would be up to the manager whether he would want to hire Sean or not.

I contacted Sean's teacher, and she responded with this e-mail:

Thanks for sending the information.

We are 90 percent sure that Sean is going to start working at a pharmacy, but I will forward this information to Career Start and let them know about the possibility.

Right now we do not have enough staff for a 1-1 job coach position, but we will call and see what we can do. Always love when families find us a lead.

Teacher

I didn't even reply to the e-mail. I called the Career Start person and explained that we were not looking for a 1-1 job coach, and I'm not sure why that assumption was made. She said she would have Sean's job coach contact the restaurant manager.

About a month later Sean and I ran into the job coach in a store, and I asked her what the restaurant manager said when she talked to him.

"I never did talk to him. I called and left a couple of messages, but he never called me back."

"You didn't stop by? If you had gone there during lunch, you would have been able to see him face-to-face. When you left the messages was it clear that it was about Sean and a job? Many managers don't call people back when they aren't clear what the call is about."

"No, I just said I was with Career Start, but didn't mention Sean's name. We already had the pharmacy job lined up, so I didn't bother to try again."

I was so disappointed in the lack of individualization and follow up in this program. They didn't consider the student's interests one single bit.

Sean did start working at the pharmacy and stocking shelves just as he had in high school. His work experience at the pharmacy began in November, and this year he wasn't behind all of the other students in obtaining a job.

Taking a Break

The world is a book and those who do not travel read only one page.
—*St. Augustine*

There were two bus routes Sean could take to his new apartment from the transition program, and Sean was choosing to take the route that allowed him to ride the bus with Ben so they could hang out each day. Ben only rode the bus two stops. Sean's neighbors took a different bus that arrived about 10 minutes sooner each day. Sean had figured out how to take Ben's bus on his own. Nobody had shown him how to go that direction. After Ben disembarked, the bus passed the bowling alley before traveling on toward Sean's apartment.

Sean had lived in his apartment for about 3 months, and one day as he took his bus from his transition program back home he decided to stop at the bowling alley. At 2:53 he turned his phone off. Life360 showed that he was near the bowling alley when he turned it off. So when he called me at 4:00 to tell me that he bowled a 170 I wasn't too surprised. I asked him why he went bowling instead of going home.

"It's laundry day."

Sadly a "caught" lesson on how to avoid housework, I would frequently find other things to do instead of housework too.

The fall semester on Fridays Sean was enrolled in a community college Outdoor Recreation class. He really liked when they learned to kayak and stand up paddle board, but he wasn't into the many hikes they went on. He had skipped class a few times.

"Sean, if you don't go to class tomorrow I am going to pick you up and drive you there."

"I'm going, Mom."

At 8 a.m. I checked Life360, and it showed him at the bus stop. I checked a while later, and he was on the correct route to the community college, so I thought my threat had worked. But two hours later, when Sean should have been midhike he texted me a photo of an engagement ring—price tag $1,799, with a message, "Please buy this for me to give to Macy."

I checked Life360. He was at the *MALL*. I called him immediately. "Why are you at the mall?"

"I'm eating Rubios."

"But why didn't you go to class?"

"I wanted to buy Macy an engagement ring."

Priorities, priorities . . .

California Girls

Life is a song—sing it. Life is a game—play it. Life is a challenge—meet it. Life is a dream—realize it. Life is a sacrifice—offer it. Life is love—enjoy it.—Sai Baba

Rick and I signed up for a Murder Mystery Scavenger Hunt in Sean's beach city the Saturday between Christmas and New Year's. It was a lot of fun solving clues with the various artwork and community landmarks in town. It helped us learn a lot more about the city while having a ton of fun with some friends who competed with us.

As we passed the beach between clues we looked over at the basketball court and there was Sean in a 4-on-4-pick-up-basketball-game. Rick was thrilled. He wanted to go and say hi to Sean, but I told him to let him play. It took him 4 months, but finally he was hanging out at the beach and enjoying the activities that were available there. When we were done solving the murder we called Sean's cell phone. He was waiting for the bus to take him the 1.3 miles back to his apartment. It was 15 minutes before dinnertime and we offered to pick him up and drive him back so he wouldn't be late for dinner.

As we pulled up to the bus stop we saw that another resident, Cindy, was there too and offered her a ride back. She got in first and slid over to the far seat, and Sean put his guitar—his Christmas present—in the car, then got in himself. I asked him, "Why do you have your guitar?"

Cindy answered, "He was singing to girls on the beach."

I wasn't sure whether to laugh or be embarrassed for him. I asked him, "Did they like it?"

He enthusiastically responded, "Yep. They clapped and everything."

What is reinforced is repeated. He took his guitar the next day to the beach to play for the girls again. I asked him what he was singing and how he was performing for the girls.

He has a wireless Bluetooth speaker that connects to his iPhone's iTunes app. He said, "I put my speaker on the guitar bag, then turn on 'California Girls' by Katy Perry and play guitar and sing along with the song."

I wasn't sure how long it would take for him to realize he can stand in one place and get people to give him money for doing that.

I asked him what else he did at the beach, and he told us he played basketball. I asked if he played volleyball too, and he said, "I asked the girls but they said they were in a tournament. So I asked if I could be their coach, but they already had one."

A good friend of mine called a few days later and told me she saw Sean at the beach, and he was having a good time. People now post on the Who's the Slow Learner? Facebook page, "Sean Sightings."

A few months later, Sean and I were staying in a hotel—we were scheduled to do a presentation the next day for an education conference. After he fell asleep I looked at the pictures on his phone and found one of him and three girls. They were posed on the Beach, Sean with his guitar, and the girls were very cute and looked like they were happy to be in the photo. At lunch the next day I asked Sean, "When you play your guitar at the beach, do people ever give you money?"

"YES. All-the-time!"

I had been hoping that had not happened.

"How much do they give you? Like a quarter?"

"No, TWENTIES."

Some people have more money than sense. Or maybe they wanted him to go away so badly they thought a twenty-dollar bill would do the job.

My son's a panhandler . . . so proud.

My next question, "What do you do with the money?"

"Buy Pop-Tarts."

Sean had become the Pop-Tart dealer in his apartments. I started hearing from other parents that their young adults were stopping by Sean's room to pick up a Pop-Tart between dinner and bedtime. He was gladly handing them out to anybody who knocked. Sean became the "dealer" and had everyone hooked on Pop-Tarts. He didn't figure out he could sell them for a profit and kept supplying the sugar addicts free of charge.

Bored, Bullied, and Besmirched

I just want to make a point that it's not just great teachers that sometimes shape your life. Sometimes it's the absence of great teachers that shapes your life and being ignored can be just as good for a person as being lauded. —Julia Roberts

Macy and Sean had their ups and downs. When she was frustrated with him she vented, as every woman does, and she mentioned to Cindy, another resident living in the apartments, that she was going to break up with Sean. She didn't follow through with the breakup, but Cindy had the information, and she was in Sean's class at the transition program, and worked with him at the pharmacy so she warned him, "Macy's going to break up with you."

She didn't just tell him once, she told him frequently over a 2-week period of time. One day I picked Sean up at his transition program for a doctor's appointment, and Cindy came out of class before Sean, walked right up to my car, and said, "Macy's going to break up with Sean."

I said, "Cindy, please stop saying that. All it does is upset Sean, and if Macy is going to break up with him, then she will do it, but you don't have to keep saying it all the time."

Cindy said, "She told me yesterday that she was breaking up with him. If she had told me not to tell anybody, then I wouldn't have, but she didn't tell me not to tell anybody." Cindy kept perseverating on the breakup. She told Tori too, who then befriended Macy.

Rick was working on the security system at the apartments one morning and went into the dining room. Tori and Macy were sitting together, and he overheard Tori say, "He did that when I dated him too." Oh boy, the girls were comparing notes.

A few days later Sean didn't go to his work experience at the pharmacy, and he didn't call his job coach to say he wasn't going. The next day I checked Life360 and could see he was still at home and not on the bus to go to his transition program. I went to his apartment. He was still in bed. I tried to get him out of bed, and he told me he wasn't going. He screamed, "I can't take it anymore." Cindy kept telling him Macy was breaking up with him. "Over and over and over. "She keeps saying it, and I'm done."

I e-mailed his teacher to explain what was going on:

I'm here with Sean at his apartment. He isn't going to work because he is avoiding Cindy—About a week ago Macy told her that she was going to break up with Sean and they didn't end up breaking up. Cindy is perseverating on it and keeps telling Sean that Macy is breaking up with him.

I've been around, and I've heard Cindy say it over and over, and I've talked to her about not saying it anymore, and so has staff at the apartments. It's bordering on bullying.

We are going to have Sean's social skills coach sit down with everyone as a group to discuss it but not sure when that will happen—hopefully next week. That's why Sean isn't going to school or work. He doesn't want to keep hearing it from Cindy—it's upsetting him.

I didn't know it, but the teacher was on vacation. She called into the class and talked to Cindy on the phone, then replied to my e-mail:

I will not be there on Monday or Tuesday next week. I will be happy to talk to him when I get back. I have spoken with Cindy, and she says that Macy told her yesterday they did break up. I have explained to her that sometimes there is miscommunication, but she cannot say it anymore. This is not her business to talk about. She feels Macy put her in the middle. We told her she didn't put her in the middle and to leave it alone.

I discussed bullying with her, and she didn't think she was being a bully. She is sorry if anyone took it that way, but . . . I see the problem is no matter what goes on in your personal life you need to be at school and work every day.

Sean is not meeting his requirements of adulthood.

Teacher

Sean is not meeting his requirements of adulthood.

I almost fell off my chair. Again, Sean is expected to have better responses to situations than typical people—including this teacher. Which made me wonder, why was she on vacation? She had the entire month of August off, would have 2 weeks at Christmas break, and another week for spring break; then another week between the school year and the summer transition program. Seriously? She has 8 weeks of vacation each year, but she's on vacation in the middle of the school year?

Not meeting his requirements of adulthood . . . How many people call in sick to work, then go snow skiing or surfing? How many people oversleep, then blame it on a faulty alarm clock? How many people don't pay their bills on time? Or have their homes foreclosed on?

What about the people putting the studs in their tongues? I was at a Starbucks and could hardly understand the Barista taking my order. All I could think was the thousands of hours Sean spent in speech therapy . . . and this guy made his speech unintelligible on purpose.

Then there are the human coloring books—people with so many tattoos that there is no actual plain skin showing. But ask them to pay for health insurance and they will tell you they can't afford it.

How many able-minded and able-bodied adults stopped going to college, live a life of drug or alcohol addiction? Or what about the ones who are so enabled by their parents that they don't even try to get jobs or move out of their parents' homes? I could write pages on adults who don't live up to the requirements of adulthood. And they don't have a developmental disability.

The sad part is this was Sean's third year in the program, and they had not listened to one of his requests, and had not supported one of his goals. They had not developed a job at a site that he wanted to try. They had not provided support for Sean to take community college classes, so he had failed two classes he tried to take unsupported. He had learned to work out in a gym, which the class had done the previous 2 years, but this year they were taking an adapted recreation swimming class . . . at the community college. So why if they could take that class, couldn't they support Sean in classes he actually wanted to take? Because there was zero individualization. I am not sure why the transition program called their IEPs IEPs. They should have called them "GEPs," Group Education Plans. Actually, education is a misnomer as well. It should have been Group Life-Skills Program. GLP.

The students in this program were all bus-trained (sounds like my dog who is house-trained) and independent on the bus. But on Tuesdays and Thursdays, the students took the bus to the transition classroom—class started at 8:30 a.m.—spent about 30 minutes doing something unknown to me, then they all walked to the bus stop and took the bus to the community college. They went to the cafeteria and ate the lunches they *brought*, because there wasn't enough time for them to buy food in the cafeteria *and* eat it before they had to walk to their class. After they quickly ate, they walked 15 minutes to the swimming pool, changed clothes in the locker room, swam for 45 minutes of the 1-hour-30-minute class, then changed clothes, went back to the bus stop, returned to the classroom for another few minutes, then left and got on the bus to return home. Two days wasted each week.

Instead, they could have met at the community college in time to take a 9 a.m. class, eaten lunch, then made it to the swimming class, or another class of their choice, then taken another class in the afternoon, then returned home on the bus after a productive day. But no—individualization wasn't an option.

Swimming class was another problem for Sean as well. Being deaf in one ear, we babied his good ear. He had had ear infections from swimming, and he was able to swim occasionally without any issues, but spending a lot of time in the pool, head in the water, was a recipe for an ear infection. So we asked that he be allowed to do something else during the class, and the teacher argued with us. We were adamant that we couldn't risk Sean's good ear, so she arranged for him to work with the instructor and do some jobs around the pool while everyone was swimming.

At 20 years and 4 months old, Sean exercised his self-determination and removed himself from his transition program. He simply stopped going, and there was nothing we could say or do to convince him to go anymore. We couldn't allow him to sit idle for the next 16 months with nothing to do each day so we requested a meeting with the Regional Center to obtain an official "Letter of Action" to deny him a day program. After we received the denial we planned on going to a fair hearing to make a case that Sean needed to be supported, and it was his decision to stop wasting his time with the transition program.

We met with his Regional Center caseworker and her area manager. The area manager asked if Sean had a diploma or a certificate of completion. I answered, "Certificate of completion."

He said, "A certificate of completion qualifies him for a day program." This was new information and a huge win for Sean. His caseworker was incredulous. She called me apologizing—nobody had ever told her a certificate of completion qualified for a day program. She had told us repeatedly that the rules stood that they were not funding day programs until age 22. She was just upholding what she had been told, and it was another lesson to us to not accept "no" as the final answer and to make sure the decision makers are involved in meetings.

Way to go, Sean, you did it!

How to Pick a Day Program

A wise man makes his own decisions, an ignorant man follows the public opinion. — *Grantland Rice*

For the previous 4 years every time there was a presentation by different agencies that provided day programs I had attended their presentations. I knew which agency we wanted Sean to be supported by when he finally gained that right.

During the presentations each agency would explain the limits they had on how many clients they could support because they had a "center" that could only hold 150 clients . . . a place to "warehouse" the clients when they weren't working, volunteering, etc.

The agency we selected for Sean has no center—it's community-based, and they have a policy—if any employee takes a client to the park to hang out, or to the mall to kill time, they will be fired. If the management catches them at the mall, it would be because the client asked to go there to purchase an item. After Sean had spent many Fridays in a variety of malls wasting time I was thrilled he wouldn't have any more mall-walking experiences. If you see Sean at the mall, it's because he needs to buy an engagement ring for his girlfriend.

This agency also does a great assessment of the client's interests and works to get them jobs and volunteer opportunities that they are interested in—not just placing them in positions that they have available. Sean's goal is to become an usher at Angel Stadium. When they do interviews they will take them and job coach him too. This agency has already placed people there and know the ins and outs of the stadium.

This agency also will support Sean in his community college classes and help him with his homework.

Here is a list of questions you can use to interview an agency when seeking a day program for your adult.

What percent of your clients have paying jobs?

Does your agency support two or three clients together and one-on-one as well?

Is there a sheltered workshop associated with your program? (If so, stop the interview here and move on to the next agency.)

How do you determine what job to place them in?

If nonverbal, how do you determine your client's interests?

Assuming not everybody has a full-time job—What do you do when they aren't working?

What kind of training do your job coaches receive?

Do your job coaches receive any behavior management training?

Do you advocate that your coaches use positive behavior supports and not punitive techniques?

Do your job coaches receive any advocacy training?

Do you teach them about disability rights?

What is the average tenure of your staff?

How does oversight of the staff work? (Do they have managers? How often do they interact with them? How long have the managers been there?)

How long has the agency been in place?

Do they ever sponsor extracurricular activities? Bowling nights, dances, etc.?

If so, is there a calendar you can see?

How is transportation handled? Do the job coaches pick them up at their home and take them to work?

If your coach has to drive to pick up my son/daughter, is that factored into the time allotted for the day? (Most are funded for 6-hour days.)

Will your program support my adult in community college classes? Help with homework?

Home Again, Home Again, Jiggety-Jig

If you want a happy ending, that depends, of course, on where you stop your story.—Orson Welles

What was I thinking? I fought for inclusion all through school and acquiesced to the school district's segregated transition program. Why did I move Sean into a segregated apartment building? All the experts warned it would become like an "institution." They told me it always does.

I was romanced with it being two blocks from the beach, and really, if I admit it . . . *I* wanted to live two blocks from the beach. After all the warnings, I should not have been shocked at what happened next.

Behavior equals communication. Behavior equals communication. Behavior equals communication. People with intellectual disabilities do not choose to have bad behavior. There is some **"reason"** when their behavior changes.

Sean chose to stop attending his transition program in January. We supported that decision. Our Regional Center (Dept. of Developmental Disabilities) granted him funding for a day program, which would provide a job coach. Typically, day programs get 60–90 days of notice when a new client is joining in order to have time to hire a job coach. So Sean had nothing to do for 60 days while waiting for his coach to be hired.

In February he started staying up late at night and sleeping late in the mornings. I didn't see a problem with this since he didn't have any place to be each day. He was playing video games in his room at his independent living apartment (ILA) late into the night and wasn't being loud or bothering anybody.

At the end of February there was an audit of the ILA by the Community Care Licensing agency . . . and we were called for a meeting.

We were told that there is a regulation that facilities under the Community Care Licensing agency that residents must take their medications within a 2-hour window each day—and there are no exceptions. Because Sean was sleeping late each morning he was missing his 2-hour window, and the auditor recommended they evict Sean.

In Sean's defense the director of the ILA asked that Sean be put on a 30-day warning to be able show that he could get up and take his medication within that 2-hour window. I tried to move the window to later in the mornings, but while the auditor was there he made the director call Sean's doctor who said the medication must be taken at 8 a.m. . . . so Sean's window was set between 7 a.m. and 9 a.m.

In March, Rick and I called Sean every morning to make sure he was up and had taken his medication by 9 a.m. He did fine until March 20th, when he didn't wake up on time and he was so sound asleep he didn't hear his phone ringing. So I brought him home until April 1st when his day program was to begin. I thought once he had some structure to his day that he would snap out of it. Interestingly, while he was home he put himself to bed by 10 p.m. every evening, appropriately tired after his day.

On April 10th, Rick and I took a long-planned trip to Africa. Sean was mad that we didn't take him, and while we were gone he missed us, and he became depressed. There were several days that he simply couldn't get out of bed. Instead of giving him comfort and under-standing, the staff where he lived became punitive and treated him like he was a delinquent. For those of you who have read the first book, you know that Sean has a sixth sense and *KNOWS* when he isn't accepted and wanted, and his reaction to feeling rejected spirals his behavior out of control.

We returned from our trip, and on April 29th, I was told Sean was being evicted because he wasn't just late but outright refused to take his medication six times in April. During this meeting the nurse on staff mentioned, "Sean has no problem taking his nighttime medication on time."

Sean has NO NIGHTTIME MEDICATIONS. I asked her what she was talking about, and it turns out when his doctor renewed his prescriptions in *FEBRUARY* she made a mistake and changed one to p.m. instead of a.m. The medication she changed to p.m. contains a stimulant . . . It increases mental processing. She was wiring Sean up, then sending him to bed . . . No wonder he was staying up late at night. He was simply unable to go to sleep.

This medication only stays in the system for around 12 hours, so by the time the morning came it was out of his system. When Sean doesn't take this medication, he has anxiety because he can't process everything going on around him fast enough. When he has anxiety he acts angry, frustrated, and depressed and will yell at people, use an angry tone of voice, and storm off. Add sleep deprivation and depression and you have a perfect behavioral storm.

The nurse at his ILA should have correlated the behavior change to the medication change. I had no idea that the medication change had occurred. She assumed I knew. February is when he started staying up late. February is when the time of his medication changed. *WHO'S THE SLOW LEARNER?*

The manager of Sean's new day program came to try to wake him up two different days while we were in Africa. He was planning on telling me Sean needed a medical examination because he could see Sean was physically unable to wake up. This man had met Sean four times and recognized there was a problem that was not behavioral, and the staff where he had lived for 7 months didn't recognize his struggle. This man also told me the staff had an *attitude* toward Sean.

He said the staff had labeled him, "A Behavior Problem."

I didn't raise Sean to be sweet. I strongly dislike the stereotype "They're such loving children." I raised Sean to advocate for himself. But like employees in an institution, they didn't listen to him. They translated his lack of compliance as a behavior problem. If he had been listened to—at his home—a place that people with intellectual disabilities should be respected, and listened to, then his medication error would have been caught, his frustration and inability to focus and lack of sleep would have been understood, and he would not have been blamed and punished.

Behavior equals communication—nobody cared enough to figure out why his behavior changed; they were just afraid of an oversight agency citing them.

I was in the process of trying to get Sean another 30 days probation period—with proper medication administration—when a new girl moved in . . . Sean was eating lunch with her, then called her a "hippo." Bullies have been bullied. Sean was being treated wrong by the staff, so he picked on the weakest person there, and we were told to pick him up immediately.

When Rick picked him up he told Sean he was going to stay with us for a few days, worried Sean wouldn't leave if he knew it was for good. At the beginning of March when he thought he could be evicted Sean was so upset because he loved living there so much. When they were about halfway to our home Rick told Sean, "You are going to move back in with me and Mom for a while."

Sean said, "Thank you, Dad." He didn't want to live there anymore. In 1 month he caught the vibe he wasn't wanted and was so relieved to leave—a 180-degree change of attitude from being afraid of being evicted.

Life Goes On

We can throw stones, complain about them, stumble on them, climb over them, or build with them. —William Arthur Ward

Sean's move home was shocking to many people. The story of how the apartment didn't live up to the dream we had of being a long-term housing solution shed light on the different living options that were working solutions for independent adults with disabilities that we know. Group homes work for some, but a couple of Sean's friends were thriving living with young couples, and that seems like the next option for Sean. One of his friends asked us, "What are you going to do now?"

"Sean can live with us, it's not like he has to move out. We just jumped on the opportunity when this place opened, thinking if we didn't get in right away, then he wouldn't have that opportunity."

"But what about after you're gone?"

Well, that's the whole reason we were looking at living options since Sean doesn't have any siblings. But it is interesting as his friends are entering their last year of college they are taking an interest in Sean again. Maybe one of his old classmates or a family friend may want to share an apartment with him when they graduate. Or we will pursue an apartment with supported living staff provided by an agency. At this time, we are all happy living together again.

Sean's job coach was picking him up for work and taking him to his job at a grocery store near his old apartment. He liked most things about the job, except the carts. I hear nobody likes the carts. He was complaining to me about his job coach . . . Sean said, "He doesn't dance and sing at work." Yep, he really did that. And he asked the store manager for "a billion-dollar raise." The store manager understood Sean and was so accepting of his challenges and held no animosity when Sean had a bad day at work. Sean has actually lived up to the requirements of adulthood, was never late, and did not call in sick one time. The part he liked the best was the paycheck. He is saving for a cruise.

Sean decided he wanted to try another job, so he quit the grocery store. He is now volunteering at a cat rescue, recently interviewed with another grocery store with fewer cart duties, he has applied for a position passing out promotional items at Angel Stadium and is being interviewed by a Reality TV production company.

He was also supported by a job coach in an acting class at community college and that worked out well. He received a C in the class, and that wiped out the F he had previously earned in the same class. His next class is titled *Acting in Front of the Camera*.

In November Sean voted in his second election. The voter's guides are a great help, as we helped Sean review the various candidates and the initiatives on the ballot in advance. Sean selected his choices, then the volunteers at the voting site allowed me to go into the booth with him and show him how to work the voting device. After the first two selections he was able to complete the ballot himself. Sean is living up to his adulthood as a contributing member of his community.

Afterword

How many adults with disabilities do you know who have an enviable life? One that you would want for yourself and your family? Make your goal an enviable life. —Ann Turnbull

When do you end a memoir titled *Adventures in Independence*? Because the adventure truly never ends. Just last night I took Sean and one of his friends out dancing to a local night club. A group of young adults encircled them on the dance floor—invited them to sit with them and cheered and shouted when Sean did a break-dance. It's a true joy to see the angels in action—how they flock to Sean in social situations.

Sean was 17 when I realized why more people don't allow their children/adults with Down syndrome to have more independence—they believed the *professionals*. We were at an event held at a restaurant and in came a 20-year-old young man with Down syndrome that Sean knew. I invited his father to sit with my friend and me, and let Sean, his son, and my friend's son sit at the next booth—independent of the pesky, boring parents. As we conversed I found out this man's wife worked in our neighboring school district's transition program. At first I thought that was great, but then my misgivings about the *professionals' prejudice* sprang forth as this man said, "He only has a 38 IQ." I almost jumped out of my skin. Here his son was at the next booth carrying on a conversation with my son, ordering his food off the menu, and functioning greater than a toddler—but because of an

IQ test performed at age 5 he was being limited by low expectations. I was so sad this young man's father thought he needed to introduce his son and prejudice my expectations about his son's abilities by spouting a number that I learned long ago means nothing when it comes to the ability to function and succeed in our world.

Please never describe your child by their IQ score, and know that no matter what their challenges and possibly additional diagnoses, that they do not have to live with you the rest of their lives. There are many opportunities for independent living with whatever level of support they may need. Plan for independence, shoot for the stars, and even if you only land on the moon, it's 238,000 miles further than you could have ever dreamed.

But a bigger question I ponder is why don't we have a Rosa Parks of the Disability Civil Rights Movement? A person with an intellectual disability who has claimed, "I'm not going to take it anymore!" I believe it is because of "Special Education."

Sean's friends who were educated in the segregated setting are compliant. They go with the flow. They allow anybody to do anything to them, and they listen and follow the rules and the directions, and they don't argue. They don't sit at the front of the bus and refuse to move.

When people with intellectual disabilities do speak up, either by actions or with their words, nobody listens. They are simply labeled as "noncompliant," or someone with "behaviors" or as a "behavior problem."

Or treated worse. Ethan Saylor was handcuffed and allowed to asphyxiate simply because he wanted to see a movie twice. The officers who treated him like a criminal didn't listen to him; they simply ended his life.

It's time we *LISTEN*. It's time we teach others to listen. Behavior equals communication. Nobody makes *you* be quiet or leave some place or make you do anything you don't want to do without listening to *you* first. Why then can't people listen to those with disabilities?

Sean is truly taking charge of his life. Sean is very attractive, he is physically fit, charming, and a huge flirt. This is actually a problem in the disability world . . . and as his father (who is also very good looking) says, "It's a curse."

Sean was at an event recently and another girl with Down syndrome was literally climbing all over him, right in front of Macy. Macy had a hard time with that. Sean is learning what to say nicely to tell the girls that he is in a relationship. His goal is to get married one day, but he has to learn that to be married means the flirting with other girls has to stop. Macy ended up breaking up with him because the jealousy was too much for her to handle.

Sean is not conserved. While many of our friends are going through the motions at this point in time we have decided not to conserve him. The main reason is the judge has to ask the person with a disability whether they are okay with their parents taking charge of their lives. I can hear Sean's response loud and clear. "Hell no." We did that. We raised him to be independent, and he won't let us take it back.

My biggest learning since Sean's birth has been to focus on strengths. IEPs and assessments all focus on weakness. They discover where the deficit is, then pour resources in to improve the weakness. It took me a long time to realize that focusing on Sean's weaknesses is just frustrating for him and everyone around him. There is evidence, in both the education and business world that building on strengths will bring more success than focusing on weaknesses.

Schools put too much focus on their students' weaknesses. If children spend all their time in remediation of their weaknesses, there is no time left over for them to develop their strengths, and in the end, all you have is a child who was really bad at something that is now mediocre at that something.

If we look at successful people, a completely different viewpoint becomes apparent. Picasso was a talented painter and sculptor, but was bad at math, and didn't learn the alphabet correctly. Steve Jobs, cofounder of Apple, dropped out of college after 6 months because he lost interest in what he was learning. Both are considered to not only be successes in their fields, but also examples of what many of us would love to accomplish on the scale they did. Both were people not concerned with improving their weak spots. Instead, they focused on building on their strengths.

Many of Sean's friends who also have Down syndrome can read and comprehend much better than he can, but their math skills are lacking. Sean's math skills have always exceeded his reading skills. Great teachers will recognize that building on strengths is more effective.

Sujeet Desai is a talented musician who has Down syndrome. He is able to play seven instruments. Michael Johnson is an accomplished painter who also has Down syndrome. Their parents focused on their strengths, and they have succeeded in those strengths.

In the long run, children and adults don't make their biggest contribution in their areas of weakness. We spent too much time on occupational therapy for Sean's fine motor skills. It was important to get him to the point where he could hold a pencil and write. We could have focused more on this strengths and interests. He is very coordinated in the gross motor areas, excels and loves sports, but at age 21 still cannot tie his shoes. Most of his typical friends slip their tennis shoes on too, and New Balance has a great pair of shoes that look like they lace, but the laces are stretchy, and they slip on. Writing is still a challenge, but Sean's iPhone with Siri dictation and spell check for texting provides the kind of assistive technology that negates those areas of deficit. Siri even reads his text messages to him if there's a word he doesn't recognize.

Pay attention to your child's strengths, point them out to the educators you encounter, and hopefully, one day, the IEP process will become more positive, focusing on strengths.

Sean has a Facebook page, and a YouTube Channel. I have access to both of these accounts and monitor everything he uploads. I have had to delete a few things, and he has texted inappropriate messages that I am able to immediately intercept. But mostly he is responsible in his social media usage.

Since the first book was published Sean and I have been speaking about his education experiences to parent groups around the country. Sean loves public speaking—which according to statistics is touted to be the number one fear of most people. To see where we will be speaking and doing book signings check our Web site at www. whostheslowlearner.com.

At this point, Sean has not attended a postsecondary program like UCLA Pathways. He has attended community college classes, and we are considering a postsecondary program and will tour them in the coming year.

Sean celebrated his twenty-first birthday with seven of his friends in a limo going to dinner and dancing. They all enjoyed drinking O'Doul's beer. Yes, there are accommodations in every area of life. But more than the beer they enjoyed dancing, and I can see that we will be going to a lot more clubs and not waiting for the two or three dances a year to be held. There's no limit to the amount of dancing now.

And speaking of dancing…after Sean moved back home he took it upon himself to rearrange our furniture on a few occasions. One day as I was getting out of my car to come into the house, he met me on the driveway. "I have a surprise, close your eyes." He led me into the house and when we reached the destination he said, "Open your eyes." We were in our kitchen, but the kitchen table and chairs were missing. "Here's your new dancefloor." Yep, every home needs a dancefloor.

Sean's activities are back to normal: Sunday mornings volunteering at our children's ministry, Sunday afternoon playing on a basketball team, Monday his job coach picks him up for his community college class—*Acting For the Camera*. Tuesdays after volunteering for a cat rescue at PetSmart he is searching and interviewing for jobs. He has applied at Angel Stadium for a position passing out promotional items. Tuesday evenings he attends his TheraDrama class at DSAOC, and was interviewed by a Reality TV Production Company. His church group *Refuge* is Wednesday nights, where they let Sean play guitar on stage—nobody tips him but he does get applause which is worth so much more. A new *Dance Abilities* Program has just started on Friday afternoons and they have frequent performances on the weekends. In the *Dance Abilities* performances Sean adds a signature breakdance that brings down the house. Cool Club and Challenger baseball and Special Olympics Golf on the weekend and at the gym he joins in on pick-up basketball games—a teammate told me he scored the winning three point shot for their team. He doesn't have a girlfriend at the moment, so watch out, ladies, he is looking to remedy that situation.

Catch up with the latest Sean Sightings or post a Sean Sighting on the Facebook Page *Who's the Slow Learner? A Chronicle of Inclusion and Exclusion.*

E-mail Sandra at www.whostheslowlearner.com

Follow Sean and Sandra on Twitter at Purpose2Inspire

To see where Sean and Sandra will be presenting, see the New Events page at www.whostheslowlearner.com

Other books by Sandra Assimotos McElwee

Sean McElwee was born with Down syndrome and entered his neighborhood school as a general education kindergarten student with the supports, accommodations, and modifications he needed to be successful. He was included in all aspects of his elementary school, learned to read, excelled in math, performed in talent shows, and most of all, made many friends. Elementary school was such a wonderful learning and nurturing experience—then the horrors of secondary school began—and sadly never ended. Struggling to be included where the students were welcoming but the educational staff was ignorant of inclusive best practices and unwilling to learn, Sean survived. High school educators limited his ability to participate by violating his civil rights multiple times, denying access to electives, sports, and elections. Sean's mother learned laws she never thought she needed to know and tried teamwork, diplomacy, and finally became punitive with compliance and civil rights complaints.

Who's the Slow Learner? includes creative examples of accommodations and modifications. Education laws unfold in this story revealing the hard lesson that while inclusive education is the law, you cannot legislate attitudes. This is the first book that chronicles a student with special educational needs from preschool to high school graduation. It is a story of triumphs and successes; losses and failures. Not a "how-to" book but the chronicle of "how they did it" as inclusion pioneers forging the way, written in the hopes that parents and educators can learn from the achievements and errors made on both sides.

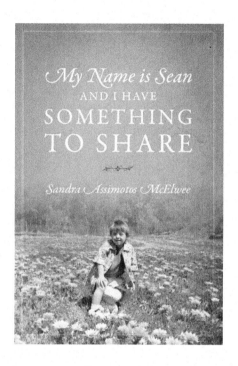

Sean McElwee was successfully fully included in elementary school with all of the supports, accommodations, and modifications he needed to succeed. This book introduced him to all of the first-grade classes and facilitated his acceptance. A great book for intro-ducing Down syndrome to peers and siblings. Explain to children who have Down syndrome that they are just like Sean. Many photos and short sentences make this a children's book that will be read over and over again. At the end there is a letter to parents of typical children about who may have a child with Down syndrome included in their child's classroom, explaining Down syndrome, Inclusive Education and how to talk to their children and even encourages them to invite the child with Down syndrome for a play date or to a birthday party.

CPSIA information can be obtained
at www.ICGtesting.com
Printed in the USA
FSOW03n0711120515
7074FS